LIKEWISE. *Go and do.*

A man comes across an ancient enemy, beaten and left for dead. He lifts the wounded man onto the back of a donkey and takes him to an inn to tend to the man's recovery. Jesus tells this story and instructs those who are listening to "go and do likewise."

Likewise books explore a compassionate, active faith lived out in real time. When we're skeptical about the status quo, Likewise books challenge us to create culture responsibly. When we're confused about who we are and what we're supposed to be doing, Likewise books help us listen for God's voice. When we're discouraged by the troubled world we've inherited, Likewise books encourage us to hold onto hope.

In this life we will face challenges that demand our response. Likewise books face those challenges with us so we can act on faith.

likewisebooks.com

Foreword by Shane Claiborne
and Jonathan Wilson-Hartgrove

Living Mission

The Vision and Voices of New Friars

Edited by Scott A. Bessenecker

Scott Bessenecker

Viv Grigg

Craig and Nayhouy Greenfield

Derek Engdahl and Jean-Luc Krieg

Christopher L. Heuertz and David Chronic

Phileena Heuertz and Darren Prince

José Peñate-Aceves and John Hayes

Ash Barker

IVP Books

An imprint of InterVarsity Press
Downers Grove, Illinois

InterVarsity Press
P.O. Box 1400, Downers Grove, IL 60515-1426
World Wide Web: www.ivpress.com
E-mail: email@ivpress.com

InterVarsity Press® is the book-publishing division of InterVarsity Christian Fellowship/USA®, a movement of students and faculty active on campus at hundreds of universities, colleges and schools of nursing in the United States of America, and a member movement of the International Fellowship of Evangelical Students. For information about local and regional activities, write Public Relations Dept., InterVarsity Christian Fellowship/USA, 6400 Schroeder Rd., P.O. Box 7895, Madison, WI 53707-7895, or visit the IVCF website at <www.intervarsity.org>.

All Scripture quotations, unless otherwise indicated, are taken from the Holy Bible, New International Version®. NIV®. *Copyright ©1973, 1978, 1984 by International Bible Society. Used by permission of Zondervan Publishing House. All rights reserved.*

While all stories in this book are true, some names and identifying information have been changed to protect the privacy of the individuals involved.

Design: Cindy Kiple

Images: foot covered with sand: ANNAMARIA SZILAGYI/iStockphoto
montage of buildings: Pekka Nikonen/iStockphoto

ISBN 978-0-8308-3633-8

Printed in the United States of America ∞

Library of Congress Cataloging-in-Publication Data

Living mission: the vision and voices of new friars / Scott Bessenecker . . . [et al.]; edited by Scott Bessenecker.
     p. cm.
  Includes bibliographical references (p.   ).
  ISBN 978-0-8308-3633-8 (pbk.: alk. paper)
  1. City missions. 2. Church work with the poor. I. Bessenecker, Scott.
  BV2653.L58 2010
  266.009173'2—dc22

                                                              2010019856

P	18	17	16	15	14	13	12	11	10	9	8	7	6	5	4	3	2	1
Y	25	24	23	22	21	20	19	18	17	16	15	14	13	12	11	10			

Contents

Foreword

When *Slumdog Millionaire* won eight Oscars in 2009, millions of Americans watched as the kids who had shown us the horrors of slum life celebrated their newfound fame. Oliver Twists in an image culture, they stood on the world stage as icons of a new reality. Somewhere between social studies class and the daily newspapers, most of us had missed the most significant global demographic change in modern history: for the first time ever, most of us live in cities. What is more, a full third of our world's population—some two billion people—now live and move and have their being in megacity slums.[1]

In his book *Planet of Slums*, Mike Davis defines a slum as an urban area "characterized by overcrowding, poor or informal housing, inadequate access to safe water and sanitation, and insecurity of tenure."[2] As a definition, it's accurate. But most of us could not imagine it—couldn't feel our stomachs turn—until we saw slum life played out in front of us in the tortured memories of Jamal Malik. A movie caught us up to speed on reality. Then the very children we had watched running through crowded streets, falling into sewage, begging for food and running for their lives—real kids from a real slum—were standing on a stage in tuxedos, grinning ear to ear and celebrating their newfound fame. The next day they all went to Disneyland. A trust fund was established, their families moved out of the slums, and they lived happily ever after.

Or so the story goes. But is the good news for the global poor really the promise of Disneyland and a trust fund?

We are both part of new monastic communities in inner-city neighborhoods in the United States. Having grown up in the hills of Western North Carolina and East Tennessee, we came to the city with questions about how to follow Jesus when the name "Christian" didn't seem to make much of a difference for how most folks actually lived. We met Jesus in people who were strangers to us—homeless friends, housing activists, Catholic nuns, the grandsons of slaves. Together, we found a way of life that gave us hope. God was doing a new thing. Here was good news.

We shouted the tidings to friends from back home and fellow students from the suburbs: another way is possible! Inspired by downwardly mobile saints like Francis and Clare, we cast off worldly ambition and embraced lives of simplicity, living among the poor. Our neighbors became our teachers. But there's nothing holy about poverty, they said. No need to make a vow, except for the promise to care for one another. Walking with friends who wanted out, we started to dream together: what could this place become if we stayed here together?

Reading the Bible in this new community, we rediscovered an old, old story. It had been there all along, but somehow we had missed it. From the very beginning, the God who is a community of persons had longed for community with us. When we failed to trust, seeking instead to go it alone, fellowship was broken. Adam and Eve hid from God. Cain killed Abel. The beloved community was fractured, marked by divisions of injustice. And yet, God did not give up. Beginning again with one family, God worked in Israel and in Jesus to bring us together around the table where, even in the presence of our enemies, God fills our cup to overflowing. This is the good life we were made for—the kind of life that lasts forever.

This is the gospel we've learned in community. But when we look around, we also have to admit that everyone is not at the table. Dinner at the Rutba House or a block party on Potter Street matter little to Jamal Malik. For the two billion people who live in the slums of megacities, our gospel sounds like a story from a faraway land. They might as well dream of Disneyland.

If our story is not true for brothers and sisters in the slums, though, it cannot be true for us. The story we read in Scripture is a global story, and the church was an international institution long before globalization. Truth be told, Western Christianity exported an impoverished version of the Christian story that has left many people believing the Good Book is a bad book and the Good News is a lie. "We have over-evangelized the world too lightly," our friend John Perkins likes to say. It's true. What it means for Western Christians is this: we can't reimagine the church without rethinking Christian missions.

This is why we're so grateful for our friends who've written this book. They represent a movement that is taking seriously what it means to be God's people in the world of *Slumdog Millionaire*. Like ours, their journeys grow out of a dissatisfaction with the promises of the stories they grew up in. But they do not end there. Their imaginations have been sparked by conversations with brothers and sisters who are living not only in extreme poverty but also in the midst of vibrant revival movements. Their vision has been complicated by strangers who want some of what they've left behind and despise some of what they've thought they needed. But most importantly, their hope is shaped by a story that doesn't end with Disneyland for a few but with good news for all, as the systems of this world become the kingdom of our God.

Our world has changed. Christianity is changing too. But our God is faithful, inviting us again to enjoy the endless journey of life together with friends and strangers who make up our new family.

Shane Claiborne and Jonathan Wilson-Hartgrove

A New Wineskin

Scott Bessenecker

It is not the strongest of the species that survive, nor the most intelligent,
but the one most responsive to change.

—CHARLES DARWIN

As a young InterVarsity Christian Fellowship staff worker at the 1987 Urbana Student Missions Convention, I recall seeing what appeared to be a shabbily dressed homeless man in the VIP area of the auditorium. The man was mixing it up with suit-clad plenary speakers like Billy Graham and David Bryant. *How did he get into that secured area?* I wondered. Later, as the guy mounted the platform to speak, I realized that the "homeless man" was George Verwer, founder of Operation Mobilization (OM). Like the organization he founded, Verwer was not so interested in external tidiness.

Following nearly identical trajectories, OM and Youth with a Mission (YWAM) drew thousands of young people in the 1960s and 1970s into loosely organized mobile communities that grew with viral speed and touched every nation on earth. Today these two organizations have a combined force of more than twenty thousand staff. Their growth is surely related to their low need for structure, their orientation toward youth and their easy on-ramps. All these things make them extremely accessible to passionate majority-world young people.[1] Mission historian John T. McNeil writes that the growth of the Celtic church in the early centuries, like the growth of YWAM and OM, was due largely to the fact that vitality trumped rigid structure.[2]

Just as these two highly organic organizations were entering the early stages of their wild and unrestrained growth, a historic event, led by the more established and structured evangelical faith community, was taking place. The August 5, 1974, issue of *Time* magazine reported on this international Christian congress named after the city in Switzerland in which it was held. The congress spawned what some would call a movement and which has become known simply as *Lausanne*. The secular magazine heralded this gathering of 2,400 Protestant evangelicals from 150 countries as "possibly the widest-ranging meeting of Christians ever held," and contrasted the group somewhat unfavorably to its theologically liberal cousin, the World Council of Churches, headquartered thirty miles away in Geneva, Switzerland.[3]

The addresses given at that gathering have resonated throughout the halls of evangelical missionary organizations for decades since. Some of those addresses openly criticized the Western evangelical missions thrust. In his keynote address, Billy Graham warned attendees not to identify the gospel with any political program or culture, a danger he faced in his own ministry. Latin American theologian René Padilla decried the Christianity exported by the United States as a gospel with "no teeth" because it left people's lives in this world untouched. The call to embrace a whole gospel, which transforms not only individual souls for eternity but social systems here and now, was eloquently penned in sections of the Lausanne Covenant, authored under the thoughtful leadership of Anglican clergyman John Stott. It stands today as one of the foremost documents of evangelicals around the world.

Thirty years later, in the shadow of that great historic occasion, I attended my first Lausanne event, the Lausanne Forum, in Pattaya, Thailand. Two years earlier, Philip Jenkins had published his observations regarding the rise of "the next Christendom," a term describing modern Christianity as a Christianity of the South, not of the West; a Christianity of the poor in Africa, Asia and Latin America, not of the wealthy Western European and North American believers whose congregations were in a state of decline.[4]

Arriving in Pattaya, I was ready for a meeting that would represent global Christianity as illustrated in Jenkins's *The Next Christendom*, a Christianity dominated by those outside the West who meet in developing world conditions, under tents and trees, possessing very few resources yet living sacrificially and worshiping in pentecostal fervor. Like the wildly successful OM and YWAM that mirrored the Celtic church's organic structure, I was ready for a measure of holy chaos and mysticism. I was prepared for an event that reflected the powerful call to a holistic gospel proclaimed thirty years prior in the 1974 congress: a gospel with teeth that affects systems and structures, lifts the poor and the marginalized and confronts the exalted powers of this world that oppress and exploit for the sake of sordid gain. I was ready for an event that pictured the global church—or at least a slice of Protestantism—which in 2004 was even more diverse in ethnicity, geography and economic status than at the time of the historic 1974 gathering.

What I entered, however, was an event that could have represented Protestant Christianity thirty years prior to 1974. What I entered was not the twenty-first-century Christianity I had been experiencing in my travels with the International Fellowship of Evangelical Students and my work with the emerging movement of workers living and serving among the poor.

The 2004 Lausanne Forum took place in a luxury venue affordable to those of us from the West. Many of the majority-world delegates, those who represent more than two-thirds of the global church, stayed in the cheaper outlying hotels. The opening evening reflected pieces of the culture of the Thai church in whose front yard we had convened, but the majority of the program smacked of the predominantly Western culture of the program committee. The opening performance featured Thai schoolchildren dressed in blazers, ties and dresses, singing the English worship songs taught to them by their North American and European missionary benefactors.

When a middle-aged, male British songleader stepped up to lead us all in a rousing chorus of the 1987 American Christian tune "Majesty," my heart sank. The "next Christendom" had not arrived at this international gathering of evangelicals. Chris Heuertz, codirector of Word Made Flesh (WMF), described what he saw at the forum—or more accurately, what he did not see: "The global Christian mosaic is younger, more feminine, non-Western, ecumenical, and poorer than Lausanne's event participants. In 2004 this global face was not the majority, but a token minority."[5]

CONTRACTION AND EXPANSION

Kenneth Scott Latourette chronicles the cycles of retreat and advance that the Christian faith has experienced in its two-thousand-year journey from obscure Jewish sect to major world religion. After growing with viral power in its first few centuries and affecting the highest levels of imperial power, the church entered a period of stagnation. Describing the disintegration of the Roman Empire in the tenth century, Latourette says of the Greco-Roman world, "Christianity had not saved it or brought it into conformity with the ideals set forth in the Gospels or the epistles of the early apostles. The Church itself was divided by bitter dissensions and the prey of power-loving ecclesiastics and princes."[6] Concluding that the church had succumbed to the earthly powers she was called to transform as salt, light and leaven, Latourette laments, "The Christian Roman Emperors were both an aid and a hindrance. The order which they gave and their protection to the Church were of assistance, but their efforts at the control of the Church often compromised the Gospel and their friendship encouraged in the Church a kind of power which was the opposite of that seen in the Gospel."[7] It seems the church had lost the firebrand energy that the early martyrs and the wild Celts had infused in those first several centuries.

Could the same lament be sung over the church in the West today? Have we so wed ourselves to the capitalistic powers of our consumerist society that pastors are more like CEOs, megachurches more like shopping malls and mission organizations more like transnational corporations peddling a product? Have Western missions created church franchises serving up foreign fare garnished with a few local accents? Where has true societal transformation been brought on by the death of a mustard seed and not simply shallow growth that counts the number of seats occupied in a particular building on a Sunday morning? Just as the good Roman emperors brought some help to the church, the entrepreneurial business moguls who write the church's leadership manuals and fund her ministries may be of some assistance. But just as European Christianity's love affair with the powers of empire contributed to its tenth-century decline, the yoking of the church to a materialistic, highly programmed business engine has compromised the gospel and brought on a season of impotence in the Western church.

But revival often follows decline, and a new wineskin is needed to hold the fresh harvest rising from fields that have become fertile during the fallow years. "From the outset there were some who caught at least a faint glimmer of what was meant by the Gospel," writes Latourette. "We must remember that the active missionaries were usually monks and that monks were those who, in theory, had committed themselves fully to the commands of Christ as they understood them."[8] Latourette goes on to speak of revival movements that revitalized the church and stretched her arms around new populations, "some of them monastic and some of them from the Catholic standpoint heretical, which sprang from a deep desire to be fully Christian."[9] Fallow ground in the tenth century had become good soil for new crops growing at the eastern edges of the empire. It was often a new wineskin that channeled revival—a renewed expression of church and mission.

A NEW WINESKIN FOR NEW WINE

Nairobi Chapel pastor Oscar Muriu spoke to the Chinese Coordination Center of World Evangelism meeting in Nairobi, Kenya, in 2008. There he spoke of how the *Pax Romana* facilitated the spread of the first-century church, just as its later cousins, the *Pax Britannica* and the *Pax Americana*, helped advance the nineteenth- and twentieth-century church. But as the predomi nantly American/European Protestant missionary movement winds down, what will take its place? Oscar Muriu suggested that for the majority-world church to uncritically adopt the Western form of missions would be akin to young David donning King Saul's cumbersome armor.

> In the new model for missions we must return to "incarnational models of powerlessness." Jesus sent out his disciples without extra clothes, shoes, no gold or silver. He told them to look for the man of peace in the village and stay with them. Go as powerless—and become dependent on those you come to save—and you will incarnate with them.[10]

Muriu suggests that rather than the heavily resource-dependent, program-oriented business model used by most Western mission agencies and churches, the majority world must use less encumbered methodologies that make better sense to Christians in Africa, Asia and Latin America. Living simply among friends and relatives overseas and building ministries centered on the slow and organic cultivation of long-term relationships comes naturally to Christians coming from the majority world. Rather than measuring the missionary task in sociological terms like *unreached people groups* or geographical divisions such as the *10/40 Window*, Muriu called the Chinese missionaries to heed Jesus' exhortation to the disciples in Mark 6:7-11 and to focus on those who are most receptive to the gospel: the young, the poor and the urban.

OM and YWAM were early expressions of a new wineskin being shaped today by fellowships like InnerCHANGE, Servant Partners, WMF, Servants to Asia's Urban Poor (Servants) and Urban Neighbours of Hope, all of whom have taken the incarnational approach that Muriu recommends and are being seeded among the dispossessed populations of young, urban, poor slum dwellers.

But neither Muriu nor the emerging wineskin discount the contribution of nineteenth- and twentieth-century Protestant mission agencies, nor that of the more historic Catholic orders. Most wines, like the older mission agencies and historic orders, taste better when they age. Time is needed for fermentation, and for the puckering power of the tannin to mellow. The wine's flavor grows beautifully complex as years mature it. The need for a new wineskin is not necessarily an indictment of the old wine or the old wineskins; it is an acknowledgment that new wine requires the flexibility of a young wineskin—new churches and mission structures capable of accommodating the new thing God's Spirit is doing in these days. Attempting to force the new wine into the old skin will only ruin both (Mt 9:17).

Some of the American and European mission agencies that grew up after World War II are full of good wine, as are some of the centuries-older Catholic orders. These are organisms with mature and complex flavor, entities with rich history and ancient wisdom. But the reformation that is going on will not mature properly if forced into the old skins. New structures and organisms are needed to help carry the new wine.

During the Lausanne meetings in Pattaya, I was in the early stages of writing *The New Friars: The Emerging Movement Serving the World's Poor*. It was there that I met Ash Barker, executive director of Urban Neighbours of Hope, a Christian order among the poor. He and I, along with others, shared some of our longings for something new. It was also there that I visited a

young friend, Dave Von Stroh, living in a Bangkok slum community and working for Servant Partners, another manifesta-
tion of this new wineskin. Shortly thereafter I witnessed the
commissioning of Filipino pastors Efran and Becky Roxas, sent
by their church in the slums of Manila to a slum in Phnom Penh
by Servants to Asia's Urban Poor. Despite my discouragement at
the ability of old wineskins to cradle the twenty-first-century
church, I was coming into contact with a new skin forming
around the renewal movements that are rising from some of the
poorest and most neglected people on earth.

I remember talking to Viv Grigg around that time. Viv helped
to found Servants in the 1980s. He was among the first to use the
language of Catholic orders in describing what was happening in
this mission-driven revival of incarnational ministry among the
poor. Religious orders are gatherings of men and women who
live and serve under a common rule or "order." But Viv warned
me about tying this renewal movement too closely to the historic
orders. "God is doing something new," he told me. "Some of it
may look very much like the old preaching orders of friars. But
we must give God the freedom to do a new thing." So in my book
I examined five historic, radically missional movements dating
from the 400s to the 1600s—Celtic, Nestorian, Franciscan,
Moravian and Jesuit. Only one of these, the Franciscans, could
technically be identified as an order of *friars*.[11] The others simply
exemplified the centrifugal signs of renewal, akin to the energy I
see coming in a new movement of friar-like zeal. These historic
fellowships shared some ancient signs in common; they were incarnational, missional, marginal, devotional and communal.
These are the very qualities showing up in a new wineskin.

What you now hold in your hands is an exegesis of these five

signs in the voices of those making up this new wineskin—
those whom I referred to as *new friars* in my 2006 book. While
most of the authors hail from what remains of the church's
Western power base, we are learning from and submitting to
our materially poorer, majority-world friends. If you want to
discover just how this new thing God is doing in the church is
being fleshed out missionally in our world, then read on. The
chapters that follow will help you to encounter spiritual renewal
as it is happening in the *barrios*, *favelas*, slums and high-poverty
neighborhoods in our world. This renewal is fueled by poor
community members who have chosen to remain in their communities or locate to similarly poor neighborhoods, by nonpoor
men and women who have moved into these communities, and
by middle-class professionals choosing to collaborate in order
to bring kingdom transformation—a gospel with teeth.

NEW FRIARS?

There are a number of ways in which the *new friars* designation
does not fit this emerging movement. First, there is the subtle
implication that the existing Catholic orders are obsolete. This
new movement is theologically broad enough for Catholics and
Protestants to work together. Far from being put to pasture, the
Catholic orders are providing inspiration or in some cases col-
laborating with this new movement.

Second, the term is exclusively male, while the emerging
movement is not. Phileena Heuertz, international associate director for community care at WMF and a recent convert to Catholicism, says that the social mores of medieval Europe would
not accommodate females working side by side with the friars.
A separate order of women living in seclusion was the only way

a woman wanting to devote herself to Christ, the church and the poor could express her commitment. Thus, orders like the Poor Clares were the contextually appropriate feminine expression of the friars. In the new missional communities, women serve equally alongside men, and they do so in all aspects of leadership and service.

Third, the new wineskin is vocationally more diverse. Jean-Luc Krieg, field director for Servant Partners in Mexico City, says the sort of transformation they are seeking in the world's poorest communities requires them to become—or at least to enfold into their communities—organizational executives, business entrepreneurs, policy advocates, lawyers and any number of professional roles not afforded the strictly dedicated life of a clergy person. The new wineskin has expanded to include in its ranks vocations that would burst the old—both the traditional evangelical agency and the Catholic order.

Finally, the so-called new friar communities are not under the authority of the Roman Catholic Church, nor have they taken vows of celibacy, two features that dynamically affect the nature of a fellowship. An ecumenical, apostolic community of families and singles serving among the poor will produce an entirely different environment than a community of gender-exclusive individuals committed to living their entire lives in a state of celibacy and allegiance to the authority of the Roman Catholic Church.

This emerging, missional renewal movement has been inspired by the ancient wisdom of the historic orders. They exist on the outer edge of the mainstream church like the historic orders, and they enjoy many of the disciplines and liturgies developed within the historic orders. What's more, they have benefited from some of the organizational, entrepreneurial and strategic thinking of evangelical mission agencies. But the fact remains that they don't fit. None of these emerging fellowships is comfortable with the word *missionary* and the baggage surrounding it.

While these communities do not identify themselves with the new monasticism, most would consider new monastic communities one expression of this renewal movement—a stationary, Western cousin to the new friars. These mission-driven, new friar fellowships have communities predominantly operating outside the West, incorporating members from Asia, Africa and Latin America. Word Made Flesh's most recent organizational gathering in Nepal required simultaneous translation into five languages in order for those in their fellowships to participate. Poor and nonpoor, local and expatriate, families and singles, social workers, pastors and professionals form missional communities in desperate places. The specific aim of each of these organisms is to plant these kinds of communities on the global fringe: places like Freetown, Phnom Penh, Kolkata, Bangkok or the downtown east side of Vancouver. They are artistic, entrepreneurial, international, ecumenical, contemplative misfits. They are apostolic activists with a vision to see the flourishing of God's *shalom* among commercial sex workers, refugees, street kids and their neighbors trapped in poverty—communities committed to work toward systemic change in the halls of power. New friars, apostolic orders, neo-mendicants: call them what you like, but they are a new wineskin into which God is pouring fresh wine harvested from the thirsty places of the planet. Turn the page and intoxicate yourself with the spirit of their successes and failures as they live out the signs of incarnation, mission, margin, devotion and community.

2

Hovering Spirit, Creative Voice, Empowered Transformation

A RETROSPECTIVE

Viv Grigg

Now the earth was formless and empty, darkness was over the surface of the deep, and the Spirit of God was hovering over the surface of the waters. . . . And God said . . . and it was so.

—THE FIRST TRANSFORMATION, GENESIS 1:2 3, 7

Over thirty-five years ago, as an emaciated university graduate-cum-missionary, I recall the breath of God's Spirit infiltrating a slum, then slums, then cities of slums, and bringing transformation. In those carefree days of youth, through a few of us, the breath began as the preached word. People were changed in Spirit-filled worship. I remember the days of healing and the deaconesses roaming and serving. I recall God's lifegiving breath through young graduate professionals learning about economic development and transforming the slums. I remember friends who were defending the oppressed and the first churches that were forming in Manila's slums in the late 1970s.

That Voice and Spirit of creation continues crying out, creating order in the chaotic pain of today's megacities, through individuals and through a new wineskin. And the Voice perhaps calls you to be filled with that Spirit and to become that voice in the world's desperate places.

A great chaos has embraced the earth as the wealthy have legalized rights to the earth's lands. They have excluded a few billion to be landless and to migrate into that chaotic in-between known as *slums*—a reality between the orderliness of peasant and tribal community and the order of the urban corporate existence. It is a state of uncertain dispossession. In the last decade, one billion people, many with chickens under their feet, have careened in overloaded buses from the rural areas to the new megacities. They are setting up illegal shacks wherever they can find space. China alone is creating one thousand new cities this decade because of this migration. This rapid urbanization has progressed much faster than industrialization; thus most of the migrant slum dwellers live without civic infrastructure and remain underemployed or unemployed. This has created an environment of disorganization and moral and cultural disintegration. Over time these new urban poor find footholds in the city, and gradually these slums regularize into thriving communities—if governments find a way of legalizing them, that is. Mostly they continue as places of ongoing alcoholism, violence and crime. Twenty-five years after their formation come waves of street children, and behind them waves of gangs and HIV/AIDS-infected individuals.

It is for these responsive, dispossessed and oppressed poor

that Jesus came to preach the good news. It is among them that he lived. It seems we should follow his command and do the same. He calls us to *mission:* wherever the gospel mission goes, people are set free from sin and poverty begins to change as new economic communities form. When missional churches among the poor grow, injustices are addressed and communities are transformed. The good news brings justice (Is 42:1-4).

THE VOICE CALLING, BIRTHING: THE 1980S

One day in 1980, when I was in my little slum house in Tatalon, Manila, the same Voice of mission called, as clearly as the voice of a child: *Go up the river and preach.* And like Philip, I went wandering, preaching, casting out demons—I had never done that before!—and caring for a drug addict. I went, seeing what God would do next.

And again one day, a Voice over coffee as I looked out my squatter window at the higgledy-piggledy panoply of galvanized iron beneath: *Go, disciple the elites at the University of the Philippines. They will change the poverty.* I refused at first, for I was called to the poor, you see. But eventually I went, and invited the elites to enjoy the hospitality of the poor. Years later, I have seen hundreds of works transforming poverty, transforming structures—many from the hands of these highly educated disciples.

Yet again, in the quiet of a squatter hut during the hours of siesta prayer, I heard the Voice; this time from reading the history of missions, for God's Voice is heard in history. I could see pictures of bands of men and women, wandering Franciscan preachers. The pictures became the basis of a document for an order, "The Lifestyle and Values of Servants,"[1] and within it, a priority for proclamation and mobility to evangelize among the poor.

As the sun beat its hundred-degree heat onto the iron roof of that squatter home in 1980, I meditated on the life of St. Francis Xavier, apostle to the poor of India, and the life of St. Francis of Assisi. It was then that the Spirit revealed to me the centrality of incarnation, communal decision making, apostolic mobility and suffering with the poor. Devastated by sickness and failure to combat demonic attacks, I waited on God in a forest back in New Zealand. The quiet Voice spoke to call the church to the poor, to write the vision down. As I wandered on a 125cc motorbike, I found a church in national revival, waiting to obey. *Companion to the Poor,* prayed into being by seventy intercessors as I wrote, touched many. Servants to Asia's Urban Poor exploded into life as a network of communities living in the slums and catalyzing indigenous church movements. Other missions followed in the United States and then Brazil, each through hearing his subtle nudges.

HISTORY'S ECHOING VOICE

I was surprised by the sound of a confirming Voice a few years later in 1985, as I sat under Paul Pierson's teaching at Fuller Seminary when he taught on the history of the Celtic and Catholic orders. From this experience I wrote two seminal papers that Pierson used with other students.[2] Around that time the creative artist John Hayes was also captivated by the scholarship of Paul Pierson, and he pioneered InnerCHANGE. Movements begin with creative women and men like John, who hear the Voice and, with foolish abandon, seek to translate word into action. They are followed by dedicated fanatics who figure out how to turn the new vision and new wineskin into reality. Capable administrators then harmonize and standardize the vision and the wineskin.

An order is a network of committed communities with common values, direction and accountability among leaders. An apostolic order clearly sees the mandate Jesus gave to the apostles to go and preach. Ralph Winter was right in his 1976 analysis of structural similarities between the mobile Protestant missions and the mobile Catholic orders. But as I mused upon the question of why Protestants were not in the slums, I realized Winter had missed some central elements. At their core, the Catholic orders are distinctly different from Protestant missions. People enter Catholic communities to find God through engagement with the poor, intercession, proclamation, community and the pursuit of spiritual wisdom. It is from these that their work springs. Mother Teresa's sisters pray six hours and work five hours. Protestants, by contrast, enter mission "teams," not communities, and then they "work" or found "works" as if they were starting a business.

While living in the slums and wondering why Protestants had failed among the poor, I realized that we must first establish caring communities, not work teams, for the human costs are high. And we must primarily become seekers of God instead of founders of works, for work will not sustain us through the traumas of incarnation. Thus, we formed Servants as a movement with aims of seeking God through rapid proclamation among the poor and multiplication of indigenous movements of churches among the poor based on a lifestyle of incarnation, community, simplicity, suffering and sacrifice.

THE VOICE, INTERCESSION AND INDIGENOUS URBAN POOR MISSIONS: THE 1990S

In response to prayer in 1988, while I was living in a *favela* in Brazil, God touched a gracious apostolic leader, Pastor Waldemar Carvalho, and Kairos was formed. Kairos is a Brazilian mission community, multiplying works and denominations in a dozen cities. There was little talk about values and orders (these apostolic workers would totally reject the idea of friars, having rejected Catholic doctrine and the morality and authority of corrupt priests), but Kairos closely matched the narrowly focused nature of the early Wesleyan circuit preachers, who emulated the early Franciscan preachers, who in turn had learned from the preaching Lollards. We dreamed together of Latin Americans in the slums of Kolkata. I believe Kairos was the first truly indigenous Brazilian mission community, and it is now one of the biggest, calling people from the slums to the slums and not dependent on the West. Each worker lives on about three hundred dollars per month, in community houses so they can pool their money. They suffer greatly as they pioneer slum churches. Kairos established a denomination with a Bible school in Lima, Peru, then in Mexico and then in Africa and China. They started a new denomination in Bangladesh and established soccer clubs (what else would Brazilians do?) for street kids in Kolkata, India. The apostolic workers of Kairos come from both Pentecostal and mainline churches, balancing the power of the Spirit and of intellectualism, as middle-class people and poor people serving together. In the West we would call them communities, but to Brazilians this is just normal extended family dynamics. "What is all this talk about community as a value?" Brazilians ask; for them, it is simply how one does life.

For ten years I sojourned in and out of Kolkata with my new Brazilian wife, spending three or six months at a time there to prepare the ground for the coming of Kairos there. Our workers experienced a struggle so grotesque that few of those who have become part of the vision can talk of it. It is a city in which only intercessors survive, in which every worker is damaged by the evil one. It is a story in which workers lost their hearing and their emotional health, in which demonic attacks were so devious that they beggar description and in which only intense prayer moved officials to place a stamp in a passport. The struggle over those years resulted in the first church in the Kolkata slums, and then fifteen cell groups. These were planted through the work of a simple Bengali disciple and his wife, a healer.

I share some of these instances of pain and hardship to say that our call, in these next decades before the King returns, must be to these most difficult cities. And transformation will not come without intercessory communities entering these cities first. The preaching orders of the twelfth to sixteenth centuries were often partners with an intercessory order of women. We need to see equivalent twenty-first-century orders of intercessors connected to these workers among the poor; in Kolkata we urged every worker to garner seven hundred intercessors just to survive spiritually.

I began to multiply storytelling consultations of slum pastors in cities. I knew from my teen years reading missions history that real apostolic speed is not going to happen predominantly with Western workers, although without them/us, many who are needed to catalyze movements to the poor would be missing. Apostolic speed will happen with indigenous leaders, many of them born and raised in the slums and leading bands of men and women into other slums.

Roy, for instance, was from Nagaland, a state of India that had experienced revival but that for decades has been brutalized by the Indian army.[3] He was a pastor of a three-thousand-member church. Touched by this call to live among the poor, he left his position to pursue life among the poor and discovered migrant workers living in a quarry. Roy began a small church, then five churches. Within a year, he had begun training twenty missionaries from Nagaland for the slums of India, forming a new mission for justice. Incarnation, or living with the people we serve, is a critical sign. Evangelizing and establishing churches is a critical focus. Working together with our poor friends to find solutions to the economic and social needs is an essential aspect of pastoral care. Roy devoted himself to these things.

Some of his workers joined a couple in Kolkata to learn how to train women in tailoring. This couple did not preach but, in a most beautiful way, kept on loving and helping until the women asked them about their Lord. Soon the whole group of women tailors from the slums were starting every day with worship and Bible study. When they graduated from training in dressmaking, they set up their own businesses that employed others. Thus economic discipleship continued to multiply hand in hand with spiritual transformation. This is inherent in true spirituality.

In the twenty-five years since writing about socioeconomic-spiritual discipleship in *Companion to the Poor*, I have walked with hundreds of slum pastor friends as we have kept expanding ways of implementing these kingdom economic principles. Discipleship is our response to the King and his kingdom. Economic discipleship involves those parts of our lives related to the material world, our living out of what we have come to teach as ten economic discipleship principles: human dignity; creativity; productivity; cooperative economics; work and rest; detachment and simplicity; redistribution for equality; management, savings and debt; celebration; and land ownership.

Some of the missional practices that indigenous workers develop are markedly different from those of minority-world apostolic orders moving into the slums (who are mostly wealthy, middle-class, educated people). The emergent, majority-world missions that rise from among the poor don't, for instance, like the word *order*, and they would never use the word *friar*. My task of bringing unity has often involved bridging incarnational works like Kairos, which are being stirred up from among the poor, with those incarnational works emerging from the West.

Generally, churches come first, becoming economic communities. Sometimes kingdom economics comes first and then leads to gospel proclamation and to church planting. This is illustrated in the work of a dynamic business professor in Manila, who started five thousand microenterprise projects among the poor. One day, when challenged that her ministry was not holistic because the gospel was not being presented, she shifted and set out to establish five thousand Bible studies, out of which have come three hundred churches. The kingdom is spiritual and economic, and in the eyes of our majority-world brothers and sisters living and working among the poor, the kingdom cannot come without the multiplication of churches. Western incarnational workers tend to talk more of mission as justice, because poverty immediately forces us to deal with our wealth. Wealthy people talk of programs and projects, which require money.

POSTMODERN LEARNING NETWORKS: MULTIPLYING VOICE IN THE MILLENNIAL DECADE

In the early 2000s we gathered leaders of both Western and non-Western incarnational movements and orders into the Encarnação Alliance of Urban Poor Movement Leaders. At our gathering in Bangkok in 2004, God spoke through a prophet of the need for fifty thousand workers from the slums to the slums.[4] All said "Amen!" So this became a goal that we would strive for, with God's help. As part of this we developed training modules on CDs and have been multiplying this curriculum city by city through "city learning networks." This has created and expanded the base of intercity relationships and resulted in many hundreds of new churches.

One day after the Bangkok gathering, I prayed and heard the Voice again. *Go to Africa,* it said. *I will provide. Go, find a cluster of pastors in the slums and train them.* I asked God to show me someone under the radar. Then, while searching online for references to revival, I noticed an obscure website about a slum pastor's library. As I read the words on the site, I was overwhelmed by the presence of the Spirit. Here was a pastor in the slums, seeking to train others with a library! What days of sweet fellowship I was soon enjoying with slum pastors of Uganda. How intense the debate between them as to whether kingdom economics was from God. From that time together, a network of missional Ugandan slum pastors emerged. They have formed three new denominations in three countries. AIDS victims have been cared for, and small microenterprise projects have begun.

Recently, when I was back in my home country of New Zealand, the Voice spoke again. This time it said: *Go train in India. I will provide.* An email from India came the next day, asking for training. Out of that venture one hundred pastors were trained, and God has indeed provided, multiplying that first training experience ten times over. Slum pastors are now being trained in five different Indian cities (and as I write, another series in another city is happening). Many new churches have been planted, lepers have been reached, widows have been cared for, gypsies and orphans have been loved and women have been trained in sewing.

"He will guide you into all truth" (Jn 16:13). That guidance can take decades to bring to fruition. In 1975, while meeting with my first community in a park in Manila, I saw, as clearly as one sees a cloud in a still sky, that movements among the poor would not eventuate without the training of movement leaders at a master's-degree level. It wasn't until thirty years later that the Encarnação Training Commission has shared a wonderful sense of unity around this vision of master's-level training. As a result, an M.A. in Transformational Urban Leadership has been developed and is being delivered in three schools. Eight others are exploring it. Colin Smith moved a whole Bible school into the slums of Nairobi, for instance, and developed a similar bachelor's-level training program.

THE MILLENNIAL FUTURE: EMPOWERMENT OF CROSS AND RESURRECTION

So here is the call: to ferment movements of the Spirit created through four phases of empowerment. First there is the *dunamis* of the preached word of God (which is the power of the gospel according to Romans 1:16); then the liberating life of the Spirit, which comes through conversion; then the growth of God-communities of faith expressed in social, spiritual, economic, political and environmental discipleship. These three lead to a

fourth phase of broader cultural engagement and transformation: derivative works, such as community organizations, development projects, urban planning and health programs, which
are all initiated by and infused with the Holy Spirit. Many more
people are needed to walk alongside slum leaders—first to learn
and then to facilitate, according to one's gifts, the various aspects of these four empowerments.

Lest you put on rose-tinted glasses, remember that along with
these great blessings, we, poor and nonpoor, Western and majority world, must be prepared to live with great pain, daily carrying in our bodies the real cost of the cross. There is daily sickness. There can be hidden costs for children of workers among
the poor who are always on the move; at times they become trau-
matized teenagers. There are unknown costs to some of our
spouses as well, who may complain very little but inwardly
struggle with the immense pressures of homelessness, chaos and
deep loneliness. There is grief at the loss of workers—a brother
pulls back from a critical work when his health fails, a sister dies
because of the contaminated food of the slum, a demonic attack
proves too much for another and all of us are tripped up by hidden sins. It would be more graphic to tell you the actual stories,
but I can't, since some of these involve living people.

THE SPIRIT, HUMILITY AND GREATER WORKS

Preaching friars? Apostolic orders? These are my reflections on
more than thirty-five years of Spirit-freedom, apostolic mobility
and transformation.

Despite our frailties and through many failures, as bands of
brothers and sisters among the poor, we have now seen these
orders multiply to hundreds of workers and indigenous move-

ments multiply to many thousands. The daughter works are reaching hundreds of thousands. Whatever God does endures forever; nothing can be added to it or taken from it (Eccles 3:14). God is the source, and God will determine the ending point of a given new mission or a new wineskin. God alone is to be praised!

I invite you to come and catch the wind! Come: dance and run with us as we speed the message of the cross. You may not be perfect, you may not be brilliantly gifted, you may not know what God would do through you, but his voice will lead you, his presence will be with you and the joy of your children walking in truth will sustain you. The following chapters tell how some of the new friars have formed the structures and signs that they share. Come, walk with them as they follow Jesus, the Voice.

3

Incarnational

THE FIRST SIGN

Craig and Nayhouy Greenfield

"What on earth are you doing?" said I to the monkey
when I saw him lift a fish from the water and place it on a tree.
"I'm saving it from drowning," was the reply.

—ANTHONY DE MELLO, FROM *THE SONG OF THE BIRD*

Breastfeeding was out. Milk powder was in. At least in our slum. Our neighbors had all seen the flashy TV ads for milk powder and had come to believe that their children would be smarter, fatter and healthier with milk powder. The only problem was that our slum, like slums all across the world, didn't have easy access to clean drinking water.[1] Many young mothers would mix up a bottle of expensive milk powder using dirty water, and their babies would soon be miserable with diarrhea. Sadly, many of these babies would soon die of dehydration, malnutrition and other complications.[2]

When I (Nayhouy) became pregnant with our second child,

Micah, we realized we had a great opportunity. Living incarnationally in the slum meant our lives were under constant scrutiny. While I ate breakfast with our neighbors in our lane one day, conversation came around to why I was breastfeeding my newborn baby girl. The local women were aghast when I told them that Micah was exclusively breastfed, and that we didn't supplement her feeding with milk powder or other foods. They badgered me with questions, but their queries soon gave way to curiosity and then fascination. The months passed, and before their watchful eyes, my daughter grew into a huge, healthy butterball of a baby. Because we lived incarnationally among the poor in this community, everyone knew that Micah had been fed nothing but breastmilk for the first six months of her life, and the local mothers were more than persuaded. From that point on, the use of milk powder in our slum decreased. Through the simple, prophetic act of incarnational motherhood, we accomplished in our slum what poster campaigns, visiting educators and government campaigns had been unable to accomplish: transformation.[3] Life!

The incarnational approach—that is, moving into a community as neighbors and friends just as Jesus did when he relocated from heaven to live among us—is integral to the missional lives of Servants and other new friars groups. Because it is so costly, however, it is important to ask hard questions about its importance. We once got a letter from a friend who was struggling with questions about a life in missions. Does the gospel call all Christians to slum living? Is life in community with the poor a "higher calling" than other models for mission? Are the good people doing missions outside the slums somehow failing the gospel, or is their work still legitimate? And is crosscultural mis-

sion, regardless of how contextualized it is, an artifact of a by-
gone era?

We welcomed his concerns. After all, living incarnationally
among the urban poor always comes with suffering and pain.
Over the past decade, we, along with our poor neighbors, have
been evicted twice from Asian slums to make way for "development." We have been exposed to the most heartbreaking brutal-
ity and oppression, and we have watched our friends and their
children die of easily preventable diseases. After six years of living in Asian slums, we moved to inner-city Vancouver, Canada—a place the United Nations describes as "a two-kilometer
stretch of decaying rooming houses, seedy strip bars and shady
pawn shops."[4] Eighty-two percent of the residents in this neighborhood live alone, and five thousand are addicted to intrave-
nous drugs.

Our friends were alarmed that we would move into such a
drug-infested neighborhood. They had only just gotten used to
us living in an Asian slum, where at least the poor were exotic
and unknown. Now we were no longer living incarnationally
among the romanticized poor, who are far away, but among the
demonized poor, who are on the doorsteps of one of our own
Western cities.[5]

Living in the Downtown Eastside in Vancouver has meant
choosing to bring up our kids in this neighborhood. It has also
meant inviting friends struggling with crack cocaine and heroin
addictions into our home. Not surprisingly, we have asked ourselves these very questions: Is it really worth the risk and discomfort? Isn't there an easier way to minister to the poor than
living among them? We've spent a lot of time thinking about
these things over the years. Sometimes our minds and hearts

are filled with doubts. Ultimately though, we must each respond in obedience to God's call first and foremost—whether we "get it" or not.

The words Jesus spoke about our mission as his followers keep coming back to comfort and guide us as we make decisions about where to locate ourselves: "As you sent me into the world, I have sent them into the world" (Jn 17:18). Did he picture the world we live in today—a world where one billion people live in the appalling squalor of urban slums?[6] What does it mean to be sent into that world by the Father as Jesus was sent?

If this is indeed the world God is sending us into incarnation-ally—or literally, "in the flesh," just as the Father sent the Son—then what is to be our role there? Is there a role for foreigners, or is mission now best carried out only by local people? In this postcolonial world, many people think we should just stay at home, live simply, give generously and make occasional trips to the developing world as technical consultants. Are we needed or even wanted among the urban poor and their slums?

A HELPFUL FRAMEWORK

John Perkins, who has invested his life in inner-city neighbor-hoods, suggests that real transformation of an urban commu-nity requires three types of people. Each of these is built on the idea that they will be living incarnationally in the neighbor-hood, not just visiting from outside.

First, *relocators* are those who were not born in the neighbor-hood but move into the area to live incarnationally and to tie their well-being to that of their neighbors.

Second, the *returners* are those who were born and raised in the community and then left for a better life. They are no longer trapped by the poverty of their neighborhood, yet they choose to return and live in the community they once tried to escape.

Third, the *remainers:* these are the ones who could have fled the problems of the community but have chosen to continue living there incarnationally, becoming a part of the solution to the problems surrounding them.

Although John Perkins was talking about inner cities in the United States, this is a very helpful framework within which to think about incarnational mission in the majority world. We will examine these roles one by one.

REMAINERS: MEN AND WOMEN OF PEACE

To understand the role of the incarnational outsider, we must first understand and appreciate the role of the incarnational insider. So this story starts not with us, the privileged minority who read English and have access to books like this, but with those who are born and have lived their whole lives in the slums and urban poor communities of the majority world. Though their own societies may relegate them to the margins, these are the very people who are central to the kingdom work God is doing in any place. Though they may never write books, speak at conferences or enjoy the applause of the wider world, they are truly great in God's economy and play an important role in transforming their own communities.

Nate Buchanan writes, "If you're *from* the ghetto, you can't 'relocate' there."[7] He points out that in talking about relocation, our starting point is too often a privileged location: outside the urban poor communities. Unless we work hard to make the urban poor who remain in their communities more central in our missiology and theology, we will always struggle with seeing the poor as "other."[8] Buchanan says, "The 12 marks [of new monasticism] lead us to a radical lifestyle, but at a closer reading, they assume privilege. Their market is middle-class Christians, and their language decidedly leaves poor people somewhere other than at the core of the community." Buchanan concludes, "It is appropriate for privileged people of conscience to figure out how we should live, but the problem is that we always end up at the centre of the story."

New monasticism provides a helpful corrective to the self-oriented, consumer-driven society that has emerged in the West. In the developing world, where the differences between the poor and the nonpoor are more pronounced, we are attempting to combat the tendency for the nonpoor to become the center of the story.

One of the motifs that has helped us in Servants to keep our focus off ourselves and on the people with whom God has called us to live and serve is found in the story of Jesus sending out the seventy-two disciples two by two to spread the good news of his upside-down kingdom (Lk 10:1-8). Jesus' instructions were clear: the disciples were to look for men or women of peace in each place. These men or women of peace were most likely people who had never heard the name of Jesus but nevertheless demonstrated kingdom values such as hospitality and compassion. In Servants, these are the men and women we pray God will lead us to when we move into a slum. These are the men and women who will be central to whatever God is already doing in that place and who will be there long after we have gone. The calling of these men and women of peace is to the place they already inhabit. They are the remainers.

Jesus commanded the healed demoniac to return home and

witness to his own family. Like this man, some who have received God's healing touch are called to remain in order to pass on the good news to their old friends. This is the vision God has given us in the Downtown Eastside, a vision birthed from a passage in Ezekiel 37 in which God asks the prophet Ezekiel what he sees. Ezekiel describes a valley of dry bones. A place of death. A valley of destruction. These words closely echo the descriptions many locals give to our neighborhood, the original Skid Row. They see it as a drug-infested hellhole with no hope of change or transformation. But God corrects that perception. He says, "You see dry bones, but I see a vast army!" And these are the eyes we have asked him to give us in our neighborhood. As we work to see people freed from their addictions, we are excited that God is choosing some to be remainers, ministers of God's healing to their former circles of drug-using friends.

Paul advises, "Were you a slave when called? Do not be concerned about it. Even if you can gain your freedom, make use of your present condition now more than ever. . . . In whatever condition you were called, brothers and sisters, there remain with God" (1 Cor 7:21, 24 NRSV).

Some describe their call to remain as a call to embrace the discipline of stability, especially in the face of either persecution or of attractive opportunities to move up and out. Jesus himself remained rooted in one place for his first thirty years; he knew what it was like to be a remainer, choosing as the Creator of the universe to abide with us, despite our constant rejection of God and his kingdom. He also knew firsthand the heartbreak of being rejected by his own people, saying, "No prophet is accepted in his hometown" (Lk 4:24).

There is a danger, however, in focusing solely on remainers.

Over the last few years, as the church has gained a deeper appreciation for the contribution the poor can make in reaching their own people and rebuilding their own communities as remainers, we have simultaneously lost confidence in what we as Westerners might have to offer as long-term, crosscultural relocators among the poor.[9] The mission pendulum has swung heavily toward resourcing local people, remainers, whose work is supplemented by short-term missionaries who focus on transferring their skills without learning the language and culture.[10]

We know that remainers can usually communicate the gospel more clearly and potentially carry out community development more cheaply than others. The foreigner then, some argue, should be merely a technical advisor, staying in country for as short a time as possible with the sole aim of imparting the expertise necessary (and then leaving quickly so as not to waste more resources).[11]

But the idea that remainers, such as evangelists or community development workers, can be trained and empowered in a vacuum, simply by a sterile skill-transfer or "brain dump," is naive in the extreme. If there is one thing we have learned among the poor, it is this: the medium is the message.

In reality, our neighbors, staff and friends pick up much more from us than just the technical knowledge they are being offered. If a trainer isolates himself from the poor by living apart, the trainee will see no reason to suffer alongside the poor when he is no longer forced to by material circumstance. He will follow our lead in placing comfort before relationship. If the outsider demonstrates the importance of living incarnationally among the poor, however, then those who watch our whole lives (such as our coworkers) will pick up the same attitude.[12]

In the development industry, in which the overwhelming bias runs toward staying in the air-conditioned office and rarely venturing down to the poor community, an incarnational lifestyle offers a radically alternative model. Likewise, in the recent history of missions, during which missionaries have lived isolated in mission compounds, a new imagination for the incarnational approach desperately needs to be sparked among those called to be remainers.

RELOCATORS: OUTSIDERS AND FOREIGNERS

The prophetic importance of this role was driven home for us when we did a review of the Servants' AIDS home care ministry, which has reached hundreds of people living with HIV/AIDS in the slums surrounding our homes in Cambodia. Our Cambodian coworkers regularly wade through mud and flood waters to reach patients in the most inaccessible places. When the evaluator asked why they worked so hard and with such commitment to the poor, our coworkers all spoke of the inspirational example of their advisor, an expatriate doctor on the Servants team who lived in one of the most notorious slums and showed the same incredible commitment to each and every one of her patients. In a prophetic "movement toward the poor," an outsider who models rather than just talks about the ways of Jesus is one of the most powerful and symbolic roles.

A second crucial reason that we will always need relocators is that every culture and society, including North American culture, has its major blind spots. These can usually only be identified and challenged by outsiders, who have been called by God to come in humility, courage, truth and love. Our pastor, Emmanuel, came to North America eight years ago as a refugee fleeing war in Burundi. Emmanuel was so poor when he arrived in Canada that he faced homelessness. But God brought him to one of our church ministries, a transitional home that provides space for refugees to get on their feet.[13] Before long Emmanuel became an integral part of our church. And, in a beautiful example of blurring the lines between those serving and those being served, Emmanuel eventually became our pastor.

Does Emmanuel, as an outsider, have an important role to play in building God's kingdom in North America? Yes! In fact, while local believers will always be central to God's kingdom purposes, every place on earth desperately needs prophetic outsiders who will bring alternative perspectives.[14] We must strive to find balance by remembering the rich biblical tradition of prophetic outsiders—which includes relocators, returners, and remainers.

Throughout biblical and recent history, God has repeatedly used outsiders to bring about his purposes in foreign nations. Born in Canada and raised in New Zealand, I (Craig) grew up with an adopted Cambodian brother and sister. My grandparents and parents have a combined forty years of ministry in Asia. But despite this international upbringing, my blue eyes, white skin and wavy brown hair immediately mark me as an outsider in any Asian slum. Truth is, I stand out like a sore thumb. Over the years I have been drawn to the biblical stories of outsiders and have searched Scripture to see whether God uses outsiders like me for his kingdom purposes in a nation.

I read about Jonah, the reluctant relocator; Paul, the serial relocator; Daniel, the youthful relocator; Esther, the beauty queen relocator; Joseph, the upwardly mobile relocator and many more whom God used to transform entire cities and nations. They could not have had the kingdom influence that was so central to their stories if they commuted. They were outsiders living among locals, and their residential addresses were critical to the roles they played.

One of my favorites is Nehemiah, who was high up in the government of Artaxerxes. He enjoyed good favor with the king, and when his heart began to break for Jerusalem, Nehemiah sought permission to relocate there in order to lead efforts to rebuild. After relocating to Jerusalem, Nehemiah worked secretly at night to scope out the city and came up with a clever plan to rebuild the wall, which was carried out in record time (Neh 6:15).

At the other end of the power spectrum was Ruth, another outsider—a relocator God used to accomplish his kingdom purposes in a foreign land. She showed up in Israel so poor that she was forced to scavenge leftovers her first year in town. The point stressed most frequently in the story is that Ruth was a foreigner (Ruth 1:4, 22; 2:2, 6, 10-13, 21; 4:5, 10). Still, Ruth the outsider came to share in the salvation and heritage of Israel.

Most importantly, Jesus chose to model this way himself. By relocating from the most exclusive gated community in the universe, embracing the culture of the time and walking alongside us in all our brokenness, he came to live among us. And he prayed that we would follow his footsteps into the world (Jn 17:18).

Throughout history God has used outsiders who have chosen to relocate to other nations. One well-known missionary example is that of a young Englishman named Patrick, whom God used to spread the gospel throughout Ireland. To make a long story short, Patrick relocated to Ireland with a ragtag team of about twelve. They learned the culture and language and lived among the people. St. Patrick's methods were incarnational and highly creative, and he sought to contextualize the gospel in ways that local folks could understand. He described the Trinity, for instance, by referring to a shamrock, the three-leafed clover so beloved by the Irish.

Throughout history God has called some to this role of prophetic stranger, because his people make a habit of being corrupted by the culture around them.[15] It usually takes someone foreign to a culture, an outsider, to see the error clearly and, when appropriate, to challenge it. Of course, we have to earn the right to be heard by first learning the culture, context and language, and also by experiencing something of what our poor neighbors experience.[16] We must first walk a mile in their shoes and learn to see things from their perspective. This is very important. We learn that when we speak too soon or out of ignorance, we are easily dismissed or get it wrong. So the role of prophetic strangers who have incarnated themselves among the poor is to learn first and then to bring new perspectives and ideas from other places. It is to agitate against enculturation and to challenge cultural blind spots.

Paradoxically for me (Craig), who sought to become an insider, one of the most significant roles I have played in the slum and in the Asian church is that of a stranger, a prophet who comes with an outsider's alternative perspective. While living in a slum community in Cambodia, we became concerned about the number of children being orphaned by AIDS. I got up in our slum church one morning, and after sharing a few verses about God's heart for orphans and widows, asked whether there might be something that we could do as a community. The response mainly centered around approaching overseas donors to get funding to build an orphanage. But I wondered aloud if there might be something that we could do ourselves with local resources, without needing foreign money. Out of that initial conversation came the Big Brothers and Sisters of Cambodia movement, which links up young Cambodian Christians with one orphan each for discipleship and encouragement. Over one thousand children have been reached and cared for by orphan ministries that have emerged from that conversation, an idea that came from a challenge to the church issued by an outsider.

The Western church needs to regain its confidence in the role of outsiders, relocators who come in humility and grace to learn first and then to offer a different perspective. This call to imitate Christ in his incarnational approach to mission comes home to me every time I see our pastor from Burundi, Emmanuel— whose name means, of course, "God with us."

RETURNERS: BRIDGE-BUILDERS AND WOUNDED HEALERS

I (Nayhouy) was born in Cambodia and survived four years under the communist Khmer Rouge regime. My father was the captain of the military police, and my mother ran a café. Shortly after I was born and when my mother was pregnant with my brother, the Khmer Rouge, led by Pol Pot, took over Cambodia and slaughtered hundreds of thousands of people, starting with the middle-class, educated people of Cambodia. Pol Pot and his Communist cohorts were determined to take Cambodia back to Year Zero, so that everyone again would be peasant farmers. During this time, my family was separated. My father and other men went off to fight, and most never returned. Women and children were sent to backbreaking labor in the fields.

I was too young to work in the fields, so my one-year-old brother and I were left alone in our house to fend for ourselves while my aunt and mother went to work. My mother tells me I was malnourished and had lots of skin problems, such as boils and the like. We moved from village to village in order to find food or to keep safe distances from soldiers.

I was five when my mother decided to try to escape. If we had stayed, I would have been forced to work in a children's work gang alongside the adults. My mother paid a fertilizer truck driver to take us close to the Thai border. We then trekked through the landmine-infested jungle and eventually reached a refugee camp in Thailand. After months on the move, we ultimately settled in New Zealand.

As I grew up, my desire was to serve God in whatever way he called me to. I also always had a longing to go back to the land of my birth and serve my own people. When I returned later to live in the slums of Phnom Penh as a member of the Servants Cambodia team, my language was so rusty that my neighbors thought I must be Japanese or Korean! But God used me to befriend and lead young women out of prostitution and into his promised place for them.

God is in the business of calling people to return, and throughout history he has used these returners, alongside remainers and relocators, to accomplish his kingdom purposes. For example, Moses was a returner, and God chose him to lead an entire nation to freedom. Although ethnically he was of the same stock as the people he was leading, he was in every other way a complete outsider. His name was foreign,[17] he couldn't speak the language of his people well (Aaron was his interpreter), he dressed funny and he looked different (Ex 2:19).

Sounds like a few missionaries I know! Yet God chose to use Moses to lead the Hebrews to their promised place.[18]

Being a returner is not like being a relocator. You are a curious mix of insider and outsider. I take comfort from Jesus' experience as a returner. In Luke 4, Jesus "returned to Galilee in the power of the Spirit . . . [and] he went to Nazareth, where he had been brought up" (Lk 4:14, 16). In this encounter with his own people, there was a mixture of wonder and anger, awe and irritation. At one point, the people among whom Jesus had grown up scratched their heads in disbelief and said, "Isn't this Joseph's son?"[19]

Family relationships are often the most complex. There is loss and grief for my mother, who has sacrificed so many of her hopes and dreams of who I would become. In trying to understand my decision to go back to Cambodia to live in the slums, my mother sobbed, "Why have I brought you out of Cambodia and worked so hard so that you would be educated—just for you to throw that all away and go back there?" She and the rest of my family want to protect me from harm, from the poverty and hardship they have experienced. While most missionaries experience fear of the unknown, those who choose to return often fear the known.

Growing up outside of Cambodia, getting an education, marrying a Westerner and working for a foreign nongovernmental organization (NGO) brings its own set of confusing paradoxes. I am Cambodian, but also a foreigner in Cambodia. I look like them but act differently. I have access to financial resources but live in the slums. I am a woman who is married with children, but my marriage and childrearing approaches are peculiarly familiar yet strangely different. I work and minister in my community. I eat with my impoverished Cambodian neighbors, laugh with them, listen to them and to some extent understand the frustrations of their poverty because I came from among them. I am one of them, yet I am not one of them.

In a hierarchical patron-client society, people are often confused about where in the hierarchy I should fit. And with my outsider's perspective, I can ask questions of them like, "Why is there a hierarchy at all?" As a returner, I have the privilege to challenge the status quo, break the rules and confront the cycles that hold so many people in poverty. I can point my own people to another way that I have found in the person of Jesus Christ.

My perspective of who I am as an Asian woman is often quite different from my Cambodian sisters. As a Cambodian woman, I suffer many of the same sexist indignities, but as a returner, I look through a different set of lenses. I am often frustrated with the structures that hold us all in bondage. In small ways I am able to influence and share a different perspective with the women among whom I live and interact daily. And slowly, in gentle and gradual ways, we are changing our futures and the futures of our sisters.

Despite the difficulties, each of us must answer for ourselves, not for our parents, the call of God. Imagine if Chinese Americans, Korean Americans or Indo-Canadians answered God's call in droves to serve God as returners in the nation of their ancestors. Most of us have the ability as returners to move right into the slums, under the radar of local authorities. We can thus model the kind of downward mobility Jesus taught and can incarnate the gospel among our own people. In the words of Isaiah the prophet: "They will rebuild the ancient ruins and restore the places long devastated; they will renew the ruined cities that have been devastated for generations" (Is 61:4).

Returners play a unique bridge-building role, and never more so than when they tap into the divine spark of creativity to communicate new perspectives to both the poor community in which they now live and the rich community from which they came. Artists have generally been undervalued in mission and even more so in community development. Yet poets, storytellers, writers and painters have historically played an essential role in activism and communication of God's heart for the poor. Our God is a creative God, and by allowing our senses, our imaginations, our minds and bodies to fulfill their God-given potential for creativity, we glorify our Creator. Not only this, but God expects us to use these gifts for greater kingdom purposes.

An artist's work is always informed by her or his experience. So, in order to speak with credibility and insight on behalf of those who cannot speak for themselves (Prov 31:8), the artist who feels called to communicate God's heart for the poor must first learn the joys and struggles of the poor by living among them. As one critic once remarked, "You say you care about the poor? Tell me their names."

God has often called us to the role of bridge-makers between poor and rich. Though not much of an artist in the traditional sense, I (Craig) have seen the power of writing, informed by experience, to move minds and hearts toward God's agenda. I have tried to use this tool, albeit clumsily. In the days after the Asian tsunami, when I was working in Thailand in a makeshift morgue, I helped the Thais carry the bodies of their drowned family members from the beach. It was an intense experience, and I felt moved to write my thoughts in an email that later became a magazine article. Moved by my words and wanting to know how they could help, people wrote to me from all over the world. Servants ended up working long-term among tsunami survivors in Banda Aceh and now in Jakarta, and great resources have been mobilized to make a difference in those communities.[20]

THE INCARNATIONAL APPROACH: BENEFITS AND CHALLENGES

So, having established that God can and does use remainers, returners and relocators in an incarnational way to bring the kingdom, what are some of the benefits and challenges in living incarnationally among the urban poor? When Jesus chose to relocate among us for a time, he experienced the same hunger, thirst and many of the same joys and struggles that we do. Why is the incarnational approach, which appears so weak and limited, paradoxically also so powerful?

One of the greatest strengths of the incarnational approach is that, by moving into a neighborhood and sharing in people's lives, our ability to build trust and relationships is greatly enhanced. Bonding, a critical factor in building trust, typically occurs best in times of difficulties, such as fires, floods, funerals and sicknesses. These can only truly be experienced by living alongside people and experiencing some of their suffering. In our slum, which flooded regularly, we experienced the smiles and friendly waves of people as we waded with them through soup-like water. We realized that an important bond was being formed as we went through these hardships together.

In Servants and other communities of workers among the poor, instead of dehumanizing our poor neighbors as beneficiaries of our projects or considering them as clients or targets, we get to know them as people. They are not statistics to us, or even the "face of the poor," but mothers and fathers and children. When this occurs, our commitment to their welfare becomes stronger. It is one thing to know the AIDS statistics; it is another to watch your friend and neighbor die of AIDS. We have found that this can be very motivating—a drive develops to do something about the issue of AIDS because it has affected you personally.[21] We are likely to give initiatives a lot more thought when they affect our closest friends and neighbors.

By spending time with poor friends and making ourselves vulnerable to the same hardships, members of our communities are effectively "walking a mile in their shoes." We gain credibility when our neighbors see that we have tied our well-being to theirs. They are much more receptive to our ideas, more likely to offer their own ideas (especially casually), more likely to tell us why a particular initiative might or might not work and simply more likely to relate to us on the basis of friendship rather than as client to patron. By choosing to return, remain or relocate to a poor community and build a friendship network there, each Servants member sends a message. That message is that we value the people and the community not just as a place to "do development or missionary work" but as a place to live. In this way, trust is earned.

Living within a community inevitably results in increased time listening to community members. This counteracts the tendency to reduce our neighbors or poverty to a formula or project. Time, combined with careful observation, leads to a deeper understanding of the reality of the poor. As Anthony De Mello implies in *The Song of the Bird*, unless we dedicate ourselves to learning first, we run the risk of acting like monkeys rescuing fish from water: operating out of our own understanding and context rather than the reality of an urban poor community. Where you stand truly does determine what you see.

Living in the community allows the new friars to observe and interact with the community at different times of the day, night and year in a way that a nine-to-fiver never could. We notice how many people are missing from the community during working hours when they leave the community to earn a living. Seasonal occurrences such as monsoon rains make the community inaccessible to nonresidents during certain months. Language learning comes more easily, too, when one is immersed in the community rather than in a classroom with a few forays into the community from the outside. And there is goodness in living more simply, having less impact on the environment.

There are challenges too. The incarnational approach has serious limitations that go beyond the obvious discomfort, insecurity and health issues. It is not a lifestyle that lends itself to large-scale interventions and huge budgets. Our organizations are small and have few people. Not many people want to move into a slum!

But that is the point, our friend John Hayes, founder of InnerCHANGE, reminds us. "Jesus incarnated to a tiny corner of a tiny country," he says. "So he was limited in the scope of what he could do. Incarnation involves deep choices that on the surface seem to go against broad impact in the immediate sense. But the integrity of the incarnational approach is so powerful that its depth eventually means the message goes wide, and it acts as a leavening against the superficialities and potential patronization of other approaches, which is very important in a postcolonial age of mission."[22]

CONCLUSION

Serious doubts are being raised about the effectiveness of the development industry, and the missionary enterprise is no longer flavor of the month in our churches. Yet God is stirring a new generation of people who want to be engaged with the world and who long for transformation, justice and relationships of integrity and authenticity. We are convinced that incarnational ministry is something closer to the ideal we have been searching for. It is time for the church to regain her confidence in all three approaches to transformational mission: to encourage and support the remainers, to mobilize the returners and to celebrate the relocators.

The incarnational approach is more than the sum of its parts. The value of incarnation lies not only in the immediate relationships developed but in the symbolic nature of the act. When the nonpoor reject their position of privilege and move toward the poor, they encourage others to do the same and model a way of life that values the poor and underprivileged.

The words of Viv Grigg continue to ring true: "In the next few years, there needs to be an ever-growing stream, a new thrust to these dirt-and-plywood jungles. We need bands of people who, on fire with the message of Christ's upside-down kingdom, will choose a lifestyle of simplicity to bring that kingdom amongst the poorest of the poor."[23]

Missional

THE SECOND SIGN

Derek Engdahl and Jean-Luc Krieg

The tragedy of our times is that while many Christians have confidence in the power of the Lord to return and change the world, many of us do not have confidence in the power of the gospel to transform society now.

—VISHAL MANGALWADI

Maria is a single mother of three. She grew up and lives in Chimalhuacan, a one-million-strong slum community on the outskirts of Mexico City. As a fourteen-year-old, she was sold by her father to a wealthy businessman to settle a personal debt. The next ten years of her life were characterized by ongoing domestic violence and sexual abuse while locked up in this man's house, guarded by electrically charged barbed wire. Eventually she was able to get free of him, but she was still not liberated. "I'm glad I was able to escape," she says, "but in reality, life continues to be very difficult. Since I'm not intelligent and have no education and talents, I can't do much to advance in life. I am a nobody here. Only the politicians and business people in my city can change things. But they obviously don't want to. So, I guess, the kind of life I'm currently living is the life I have to accept and bear. There's not much else I can do. Why hope for a better future, when I will be disappointed anyway?"

Everyone has a story. We have all experienced hope, fear, triumph and tragedy. Like Maria, we may also realize that our individual narratives are shaped by the larger story we believe we are part of. Unfortunately, for many people that story is dominated by suffering, fatalism and despair. Maria's life is almost unimaginable to many of us. Most of us have never even known anyone who has suffered like her, let alone experienced it ourselves. But tragically, her story is not unique. We're living in a world where one out of six people lives in an urban slum. In just twenty years, that number will have increased to one out of every four people. Aside from clean water and AIDS, the issue of ongoing, rampant urbanization is one of the greatest challenges of the twenty-first century and of our generation. According to the World Bank, "urban poverty will be the most significant and politically explosive problem of the [twenty-first] century."[1] In other words, urban poverty will increasingly have regional and global ramifications. The way we respond to it will determine the future of our world.

THE CHALLENGE FOR MISSIONS

The global church is not ignorant of these trends and has made some significant efforts to address them. Yet, truth be told, churches in general have made little transformative impact on their surroundings. Even though since the 1970s there have been the highest numbers of new converts and church plants in world history—especially in the evangelical/Pentecostal/ charismatic wing of the church[2]—and even though there have never been more professed Christians or more churches in all of world history than today, the places where this growth is occurring are countries of growing brokenness, political instability, corruption, material poverty and disease. The Philippines, Nigeria, Haiti, Kenya, Nicaragua, Guatemala, Zambia, Rwanda— the list could go on! While the church worldwide has done a commendable job of doing what she set out to do—evangelize, save souls for heaven and plant churches[3]—the slogan "Change people, change society" has not always proven to be true. Data show that higher percentages of Christians in a country do not necessarily translate into more just and moral societies.[4]

Yet, if God intends his church to be the principal instrument to advance his kingdom's agenda, we would expect to see the growth of the church linked to evidence of the kingdom's presence. This presence liberates people spiritually, physically, socially, economically and politically, since these forces can keep a person in bondage. Historically, where there have been advancements in quality of life, the church has been involved. The church was a major force in establishing political freedoms, abolishing slavery, creating hospitals and centers for higher education, advancing the civil rights movement in the United States and ending apartheid in South Africa. Without diminishing the suffering caused by the church during the Crusades, Inquisition and the West's colonial rule, we may not fully realize how horrific the present world would be without the redeeming effect of church over the past two thousand years. And yet today there seems to be only modest evidence of Christians being salt and light in their cities and nations, particularly in the area of poverty. Given the sheer number of people in the world who claim Jesus as Lord, one would expect more. So why has the church had such limited transformational impact on the world around it?[5] While there may be many answers to this question, could it be that, in some significant way, we have not been telling and living the whole story of God's desire to redeem the earth?

WHAT KIND OF STORY ARE WE TELLING?

Ivan Illich, the philosopher and social theorist, was once asked, "What is the most revolutionary way to change society: Is it violent revolution or gradual reform?" He gave a careful but very insightful answer: "Neither. If you want to change society, then you must tell an alternative story."[6] The church has the most revolutionary story in the history of humankind, but for some reason we continually fail to tell it in all of its dimensions and to live in its reality. Instead, we settle for alternate realities and lesser visions that in the end fall far short of that which God would have for us. Mahatma Gandhi once commented on this when he said: "You Christians look after a document containing enough dynamite to blow all civilisation to pieces, turn the world upside down and bring peace to a battle-torn planet. But you treat it as though it is nothing more than a piece of literature."[7] Indeed, it seems that a significant number of Christians have accepted Christianity as a religious belief system—a little Jesus to spiritualize their life and a little extra God to give them peace in a stress-filled world. But they have not allowed the biblical message to transform their underlying worldview, the framing narrative or storyline that continues to shape the way they really live their lives.[8] In doing so, they have shrunk the gospel to a confined system of propositions, rules and pet doctrines in lieu of teaching Scripture as an epic of inestimable scope and depth that tells us about the overarching story in which we've been called.

People need Jesus. But they need the Jesus who lived and lives in God's larger narrative, not just a set of theological beliefs. Scripture tells us a story that has the ability to transform individuals, to lift communities out of poverty and to build nations that are free, just and compassionate.[9] It's a story powerful enough, good enough and hope-filled enough to overcome the destructive worldviews, societal patterns and cultural narratives from which our globe suffers. These narratives are steeped in meritocracy, resignation, cynicism, naiveté and complacency. Scripture's story not only addresses spiritual and emotional concerns but societal and systemic ones too. We need to rediscover *this* story for our own lives, and then we have to go out and tell it.

WHAT IS OUR STORY?

In the beginning God created the heavens and the earth. He created people in his image—people with dignity, worth and purpose. He gave those people authority over the earth and the life on it. There was *shalom*. The Hebrew word is often translated "peace" in English, but it contains a much larger idea of prosperity, justice, well-being and completeness.[10] God created a world and made human beings stewards of it with the intention that they would establish his purposes by promoting good, just, peaceful and lifegiving relationships within all of creation. In the garden humans had unity with God and unity with the rest of the created order.

Tragically, the *shalom* for which we were all created was short-lived. The man and woman became convinced that God was holding out on them, and they chose to distrust God and know evil. As a result, all their relationships broke down: their relationship to God, each other and the world. Violence, injustice, control, discrimination, oppression, exploitation and deprivation crept in as a result of that first breach of trust. Such things are so much a part of our current reality that it can be difficult to envision a world without them. But poverty, suffering and death were never intended for us. They are as foreign to who we were created to be as cancer is to the human body. They feed on us, choking out the life we were meant to have. It may be hard to imagine a disease-free world because all we have ever known is illness. But it is not as it was intended to be.

Despite our rebellion, God did not abandon his creation. Out of this fallen world he called a new man and woman and made their descendants into a chosen nation: a people who would be blessed by God and make God's heart for justice and peace come alive in their life together. God intended that the nation of Israel show the world his truth and advance his vision of *shalom* on earth. Like Adam and Eve, however, they too failed to live fully in the purpose God had for them. Prophets warned them to repent, to honor God, to seek justice and to care for the poor and vulnerable, but they did not. And judgment fell on them, like it did on their first parents.[11]

But then God himself entered our story. The Word became flesh and dwelt among us. Jesus began to preach the good news of God's kingdom, which he contrasted with the empires of our world. In the kingdom of God, he expanded upon the idea of *shalom*. It was to be a place not only where there was no murder but no hatred, not only no adultery but no lust, not only justice but sacrificial generosity toward the needy. Not only could human beings be God's people, but by Jesus' sacrifice they could become his adopted children. Jesus taught his followers to pray that God's kingdom would come on earth as fully as it is in heaven. He also called them, and empowered them with the Holy Spirit, to become a new people set apart to live out the values of God's kingdom in the world.

Jesus' death and resurrection liberated those of us who believe in him from the grip of sin and death. Because of this we can all experience freedom, even those who are still imprisoned in poverty and oppression. But that does not mean that Jesus' work on the cross only frees us spiritually or that our physical freedom is inconsequential. He also liberated the entire creation from the evil powers and oppressive structures that continually oppose God's kingdom vision of *shalom* (Eph 1:15-23). All authority in heaven and on earth has already been given to Jesus. His reign is present even though it has yet to come in fullness. So today, Jesus sits above all powers, principalities, systems and structures of this world, preparing for the time when his reign will be fully established on earth as it is in heaven. He will root out death, and the earth as we know it will be saved from decay, corruption and evil domination. It will be transformed into a universe filled with *shalom* as Jesus has revealed it.

The great drama will not end, as some have imagined, with "saved souls" being snatched up into heaven, away from the wicked earth, where they will sit on clouds and play harps forever. The end of the story is much like the beginning, with the creation of a new heaven and a new earth. It will not be completely destroyed and then rebuilt, however, but it will be re-created into what it has always groaned to be: a place of justice and peace, where God, people and creation are reunited, where we will see God face to face and worship him and the Lamb forever. It will end with the New Jerusalem coming down from heaven to earth and God making his dwelling place among us on earth. Our first parents were formed out of the muddy flesh of the earth. We are part of it, and it is part of us. This is our final home, not heaven.

This is the biblical vision of salvation and redemption.[12] God's story concludes with his people reassuming their roles as priests and regaining their authority and dominion over this earth. Then we will discover that it is not the end of the story but really only the beginning: chapter one of the great story that no one on earth has read, that goes on forever and in which every chapter is better than the one before.[13]

OUR CALL TO TRANSFORMATIONAL MISSION

When I (Derek) read a novel, I often jump to the last page to read the final sentences. I find it fascinating to know the end and discover how the author gets there. I understand that this approach would spoil it for some people. The denouement is ruined, they might argue, if you skip the story that builds up to it. In the case of the larger narrative in which we live our lives, however, it is essential that we know the ending, because the "end" helps us understand the plot line of the present. We know the final sentence. The only question is how we get there.

According to Jesus' vision, the purpose of the church is to worship and adore, pray and heal, teach and equip, reconcile and be in community, be the hands and feet of God on earth, proclaim God's story and make disciples, serve and do good works and seek justice for the oppressed and voiceless. It seems then, based on Scripture, that the assembly of Jesus' followers is the centerpiece of God's plan to redeem this world. God in his wisdom has chosen to work through people. Despite our frailty and wandering hearts, he continues to call us to become new creations working toward a new creation. Throughout the centuries the church, like Israel before it, has certainly made many mistakes and failed to fulfill its purpose. Whenever the church has abandoned God's vision of *shalom*, the results have been somewhere between disappointing and horrifying. When the church has accepted its calling, however, people and entire communities have been transformed by God's power. We are part of God's story, and he continually calls out to us to join in his work of transforming the world.

Chris and Maggie Rattay moved into a poor Latino neighborhood in East Los Angeles as part of a partnership with Epicentre (a Chinese American church) and Servant Partners. Chris began to hang out with the local high school football team where he met one of the team mothers, Lucy Robles. Lucy was a formidable woman; she was soft-hearted, but she also spoke her mind with expletive-laced clarity. The kids respected and loved her. Lucy had a passion to save the young people in her community. She saw the temptations that afflicted them. She witnessed many of them lose their lives to addiction and violence. But she bore her own pain as well, having grown up in poverty and abuse in Mexico and struggling to survive as an immigrant. As she and Chris built a friendship, she poured out her life and the pain she had experienced. He assured her that Jesus could heal her pain and asked if she wanted to learn more about him. Chris remembers sitting in her home and sharing about the gospel and God's vision for *shalom*. Lucy decided that she needed Jesus, and her life became renewed. Her understanding of God had been limited to ritual and superstition. But as Chris opened up the Scriptures to her, she found a real person in Jesus—one who could be in relationship with her and who could offer her healing.

She was equally excited about the teaching that God wanted her to seek *shalom* for her entire community. "We have to tell everyone about this," she told Chris. Almost immediately, she took what she had learned and began to share it with the Spanish speakers in the neighborhood. She joined the house church that Chris had started, but because of her outreach she was soon leading her own new group. Chris continued to launch new groups, and after a while they had a network of four house churches. The four communities decided that they wanted to become a larger worshiping body, and Lucy was commissioned to lead the new church's efforts to work for the transformation of the neighborhood.

Chris and Lucy's partnership is wonderful to watch. Their affection and respect for each other is obvious. They come from such different backgrounds, yet they have found unity in their love of Jesus and their dream for what their community could become.

WHAT IS TRANSFORMATION?

The word *transformation* is thrown around a great deal these days. When we talk about transformation, we mean the ever-increasing realization of the kingdom of God in a particular community of people in a specific geographic area. This kind of transformation makes it possible for people to live the fullness of life that God promised us here on earth. It is based in visible changes that positively affect the circumstances of individuals, communities and even systems. In order to envision and then implement this better future, however, the poor and the non-poor alike need to experience the restoration of their true identity and recover their true vocation. This can only happen when people begin to understand that God calls them to integrate their story into his story.

Correspondingly, Christian witness must be intrinsically interrelated with the whole transformational process. Without Christian witness, as witness-in-word, witness-in-life, witness-in-deed and witness-in-sign, sustainable transformation is simply not possible. People cannot recover their true identity and vocation apart from a restored relationship with God through Jesus Christ. The kind of transformation we're seeking, then, cannot be manufactured but depends on God's miraculous intervention. It depends on his Spirit-empowered people to proclaim his story, and, accompanied by signs and wonders, to inspire people with hope and then to gather them into new communities of faith. As God frees people from an unhealthy focus on simple survival and acquisition of more material goods to a life of service and love of neighbor, transformation begins to occur. Growth in their capacities to shape their own lives, neighborhoods and physical environments in harmony with the purposes of God produces an ever-greater expression of justice and peace.

With this in mind, we think it is important to distinguish such *holistic community transformation* from what has traditionally been called *community development*. The latter normally uses the lifestyles, values and structures of the so-called developed world as its goals for development, and it is normally not concerned with issues of spiritual and worldview change. Those of us working with a community transformation model, however, will not only facilitate physical, economic and skills development. We will also insist on developing the spiritual depth and strength of a community, precisely because we believe that the truth of God's kingdom can set people free. We will seek a kind of economic and social development that is appropriate to, and affirming of, the existing cultures of the people with whom we partner and work. In addition, where there are structural inequities that damage the lives of individuals, families and neighborhoods, we will enter the public arena as advocates who effect structural change.

In Servant Partners, we have broken down these general ideas about transformation into eight categories. Together they give us a concrete vision of what we are praying for and working toward.

1. Reproducing transformational communities of people following Jesus. When people come into a real relationship with Jesus, they and their relationships are changed. The exact structure of such communities is less significant to us. It does not matter if they are small house churches or larger institutional churches. At the heart of any transformation must be a community of people who are committed to living under the lordship of Christ.

2. Increased civic participation for the common good. It is important that the victims of poverty and oppression find their voice in order to see their communities become what they envision and not what those outside of their community want. No society can be transformed until the vulnerable have the ability to address the needs of their neighborhood.

3. Improved accessibility to education that equips and enhances life. Education is a powerful tool to help people out of poverty. Not all education, however, empowers and frees people. Good education has to develop the unique strengths of individuals in such a way that they can take charge of their own lives.

4. Expanded opportunities to achieve economic sufficiency. Those who are poor need access to economic tools that allow them to provide for the basic needs of their families. This may come in many forms—from loans for building individual businesses to larger job creation schemes that spur the technological and industrial development of slum communities.

5. Increased spiritual and psychological health and freedom from destructive patterns. Addiction, the occult and unhealthy lifestyles have particularly strong grips on poor communities. In order to become what God has created them to be, people need to be liberated from those things that strangle the spiritual and mental life out of them.

6. Increased family health and well-being. A transforming community helps families free themselves from domestic violence, sexual abuse, divorce, teen pregnancy and other destructive patterns. Healthy families are the building blocks of any community.

7. Improved environmental and community health. A community must also address those conditions that oppress its physical health. Every community deserves a healthy environment, clean neighborhoods, beautiful spaces and access to decent, affordable health care.

8. Presence of political, economic and legal systems that work for the poor and vulnerable. Many people will not be freed from the grips of poverty if larger systems are not also transformed, allowing them to live lives of dignity. Unless the systems themselves are confronted, people will continue to be victimized by the wealthy and powerful status quo. They will continue to be blocked from economic sufficiency, their desires for their lives will be crushed, and they will be vulnerable to oppression and labor exploitation, including the sex industry and government corruption. What begins with the transformation of the individual must extend to the larger collective arena that so affects the individual's life.

OUR PART IN GOD'S STORY

The story God has entrusted us to proclaim and live out is powerful. It is capable of redeeming even the most difficult lives. Our friend Ema was born into poverty in the massive urban sprawl that is Manila in the Philippines. When she was young, her family rented a house in a squatter community called Balic Balic, which was built illegally around the local train tracks. Houses were built so close to the tracks that sometimes the trains would scrape their roofs. Ema's family of five lived in a house of about twenty-five square feet. Since they had no running water, they made a daily trek to a communal faucet and had to use a communal bathroom some two hundred yards from their home. Her father was an alcoholic and gambler and unable to keep a job. He would often steal his children's school lunch money to feed his addictions. Rather than a help, he was a drain upon the family, a fact that led to a lot of conflict between Ema's parents while she was growing up.

Ema was eleven years old when International Teams moved into the community to start a church. Her mother became the first convert. Ema and her sister followed soon after. In Jesus she discovered a different story. In the missionaries she saw the love of Christ fleshed out. When her parents abandoned the three children for a week, the missionaries took care of them. Although Ema had done very well in high school, because of her family's poverty she had never imagined that she would get the chance to go to college. Scholarships were based on merit, not need. But an American man who had visited the ministry decided to help her financially so that she could enroll in college, and once enrolled, she excelled in her classes, which allowed her to get financial assistance for the next couple of years. She ended up marrying an American, Aaron Smith, who had come to study and live among the poor.

Now Ema had all the resources to escape poverty. Jesus had helped her to survive the chaos of her family. She was college-educated and married to a Westerner who could take her back to the United States to live in comfort. But Ema and Aaron decided that the people in Balic Balic still needed to know Jesus and his power to transform lives. They decided to stay in the community, working with the neighborhood church in which she grew up and with Servant Partners in training new staff and interns.

You could feel the difference that the presence of their Christian community made in Balic Balic. Despite their great poverty, people gathered throughout the week to worship in joy and gratitude in the little church building on the tracks. The area immediately around the church was noticeably free of the drug use and violence that existed only a couple hundred yards away in either direction. It was as if the hope within the body of believers held the despair at bay. Parents used Ema as an example for their children of what was possible for their lives. They did not need to turn to drugs and alcohol to numb their hopelessness, and prostitution and crime were not their only means for economic advancement. Ema's life proved there was another way.

In 2008, the government tore down Balic Balic to make way for a newer train system. The squatter community was fifty years old, and for many it was the only home they had ever known. Thousands of people were displaced, and the church building that had been the rock at the center of the neighborhood was destroyed. The community of believers was dispersed throughout the city. Ema and Aaron moved to a new poor community in another part of Manila. In 2009 they started a new house church in a room above their home, with the desire that it would be a source of hope in the new neighborhood. Ema's transformed life continues to offer the hope of transformation to those around her.

Few would doubt that the gospel can change lives, but in Ema's and Lucy's cases, it required people going and living with them in their story. People had to be willing to endure poverty in order to bring hope to the impoverished. Jesus proclaimed good news to the poor, but so few of us are willing to follow in his footsteps. The costs seem too high. Our love of wealth and comfort has dulled our senses to the needs of others. We have not been generous or merciful. Somewhere we stopped teaching that we need to lose our lives to gain them, and we decided that wealth and worldly success are not the enemies of the kingdom that Jesus taught that they were. We settled for a shallow version of discipleship and stopped believing and praying for God's kingdom to come on earth. The church has remained irrelevant in large parts of the urban world precisely because a majority of its members has settled for a much lesser vision and a much lesser story by which to live their lives. It's no wonder, then, that we're not making any transformative impact on our cities as a whole. Instead, we give authority to storylines that are simply out of touch with God's purposes.

In order to see transformation in the world, particularly in the area of poverty, we have to do three things. First, we have to know the story of those who are suffering. Then we have to believe both that transformation of individuals and communities is possible and that it is God's will. Finally, we have to roll up our sleeves and, with God's help, integrate our personal stories into God's story and work toward such transformation.

GOD SAVES MORE THAN SOULS

It is true that the kingdom of God will never come fully until Jesus returns. In the last days the New Jerusalem will descend from heaven, which implies that is not made by humans on earth.[14] But the fact that our efforts will never achieve perfection does not mean that we should not be moving toward God's intention for us. If God expected Israel to live out *shalom*, why should his church—having witnessed the life, death and resurrection of Jesus Christ and having been reconciled to the Father and empowered by the Holy Spirit—have less expected of her? In fact, we are called to something even greater than what Israel ever dreamed. If we limit the work of the church to saving souls, we have missed the point of the story.

Indeed, if we want to care for our poor brothers and sisters, we must believe that transformation is possible not only on an individual level but also on a societal level. This means that we will need to address the systems that keep them in poverty. Doing so is really only an extension of what it means to love our neighbors as ourselves. If we want to have enough food to eat, enough work to sustain us and enough access to education and good medical care, then we should work to see that our sisters and brothers have access to the same. If we want to live in a just society free of oppression and prejudice, we should work to see that our sisters and brothers can live in the same. Failing to act is a decision to bless the evil that befalls those in suffering. Martin Luther King Jr. once said: "We must learn that passively to accept an unjust system is to cooperate with that system, and thereby to become a participant in evil."[15] Thus he concluded, "We will have to repent in this generation not merely for the hateful words and actions of the bad people but for the appalling silence of the good people."[16]

When you consider the great deal of poverty, suffering and oppression in the world, it would be natural to ask why God has allowed such evil to prevail in his creation. It is a large question that would require more theological reflection than we have space for here. But the fact that God has allowed such suffering should not lead us to believe that he is indifferent to it or that he does not intend to limit its presence in the world. His plan to deal with suffering is to create a people who live as citizens of his kingdom on the earth. We are to be salt and light in an insipid and dark world. At this point in the story, we who follow Jesus are participants in God's answer to the world's brokenness. Eventually the promise is that God himself will wipe away our tears, but in this life he calls us to be his hands and feet. If all Christians lived out Jesus' commands to live simply and care sacrificially for their poor brothers and sisters, there would be much less poverty in the world. Poverty exists not because God does not care but because we do not. It exists because we continually edit out large chunks of the divine story that we don't want to respond to. Our efforts to see God's kingdom come will always be imperfect. But we will never know what can be done until we get out of our Sunday morning seats and try.

A STORY POWERFUL ENOUGH TO TRANSFORM EVEN CITIES

El Carmen de Bolívar is a city of roughly one hundred thousand inhabitants in the heart of Colombia's armed conflict. Sustained war activities over the course of the past few decades have had huge political, social and economic effects in the city. Forced displacements broke the social fabric, and basic services are lacking throughout the city. Almost three-fourths of the population live in poverty, and during the height of the conflict, many had trouble finding enough food to eat. While the severity of the armed conflict has abated over the course of the past three to four years, poor urban governance and blatant corruption continue to hinder the population from living in just and dignified conditions.

Initially, the city's fifteen evangelical churches did not feel the need to address the conflict. Only when pastors from the surrounding region were murdered and hundreds of church members displaced did the church leaders from El Carmen begin to think that something needed to be done. Apart from offering temporary shelter to displaced families, however, they failed to consider concrete and long-term strategies to address the situation.

Edilberto and Elena, assistant pastors at one of these churches, finally felt the need to break out of their congregation's traditional way of doing things. Encouraged by a sense of God's call, they started a new church plant in 2001 to aid displaced people and present a more holistic gospel to their poverty-stricken neighbors.

They also began the process of starting their own nongovern-mental organization, ASVIDAS, in order to sustain the small community-organizing projects that Elena had launched.

Elena's tireless efforts to encourage neighbors and commu-nity leaders to address flagrant public mismanagement of funds eventually brought together fourteen civic groups. They dis-cussed a concerted course of action and initially created a proj-ect that attained food security for 350 peasant families. But they did not stop there. They began to challenge the assumption that nothing could change because of the political giants in the land. "I know that what we're doing is dangerous," Elena has said, "since we're upsetting the status quo. But I continue with this work because I want to help improve the economic and political situation of my people; but most of all because God calls us to seek the *shalom* of our city. I take a lot of courage and inspira-tion from Jesus himself, who was willing to confront the powers of his time in order to lay open the injustice of their governance. As a follower of Jesus, I need to follow him in this area too."

In the last few years, ASVIDAS has helped build the network of social organizations for human rights into a platform com-posed of forty-two civic groups; by working together, they in-crease their influence in the city. Because of this they were able to participate in the city's development plan, during which they pressed the government to address issues of health care, im-proved housing and higher-quality schooling. They even offered a six-month course in human rights administration, in which they trained community members to work for social change. For the first time the voices of the suffering and destitute are being heard in the halls of power.

There is still a great deal to be done, but Elena hopes that building a network will allow them to become better equipped and more powerful in holding public officials accountable. Despite the obvious dangers involved in this undertaking, Elena and her group press forward to see the kingdom come in their city. "The beauty of all of this," she has said, "is that we, as the church, have been able to significantly improve our standing with other civic groups. Some community leaders have either found or renewed their faith in God as a result. I really pray that many more churches will get involved and reproduce our experience in other cities." Because Elena's vision of the mission of the church was not too small, a city is being changed. If it catches on, a country could be changed.

JOINING OUR STORIES WITH GOD'S STORY

Working for transformation is not easy. There are many setbacks and disappointments. Change agents are a threat to the power of the establishment; because of this, they are often the victims of its wrath. Even when a majority wants change, there is always a powerful minority that will fight to maintain the status quo. In addition, transformation often takes much longer than we have the patience for. We often have to think in terms of generations, not years. It necessitates investment in local leaders, which can take time. So many people want things to happen quickly and dramatically, but real change requires perseverance. Even Jesus' first followers seemed to assume he would be returning soon, but he did not. We need to be prepared for Jesus' imminent return, but we must plan that he will be delayed. Martin Luther, the reformer, thought of it this way: "Were the world to end tomorrow, today I'd plant an apple tree."[17]

We are all still under the Great Commission: to proclaim the gospel and teach people to obey all that Jesus has taught us. That commission does not just apply to the Western church but also to our brothers and sisters in Asia, Africa and Latin America. It does not just apply to the rich but to the poor as well. Nor should the rich or Western church be excluded from the call because of past mistakes or fears of domination. As Craig and Nay Greenfield argue in their chapter on incarnation, there is still an important role for the outsider, whether that be someone from another culture or another class. The call to mission is a call to the church universal.

With this said, how we respond together as a global church to the challenges of rampant urbanization and oppression and suffering will heavily depend on the framing narrative by which we live our lives. Some narratives will lead us to resignation, cynicism, indifference or complacency as a way of self-protection. God's story, however, can give us the hope, the faith, the direction and the stamina to fight for the seemingly impossible. That's why it is so important that we, as followers of Jesus, embrace, proclaim and live this story—a story that has the power to liberate people in the fullest sense. This is the mission of the church. This is our mission! If we all weave our stories into God's story and seek *shalom*, if we all live out the kingdom to the best of our Spirit-empowered abilities, twenty-second-century historians may write about a powerful movement of communities of Jesus' followers that emerged in the beginning of the twenty-first century. They may write about a movement that helped turn the tide against the slumification of our planet and that contributed to the transformation of our cities.

Marginal

THE THIRD SIGN

Christopher L. Heuertz
and David Chronic

The truth is, however, that the oppressed are not "marginals," are not people living "outside" society. They have always been "inside"—inside the structure which made them "beings for others." The solution is not to "integrate" them into the structure of oppression but to transform that structure so that they can become "beings for themselves."

—PAULO FREIRE, *PEDAGOGY OF THE OPPRESSED*

During the last Christmas season, staff from our Word Made Flesh (WMF) children's home in Chennai, India, found a brother and sister living and working on a trash heap. Referred to as *rag-pickers*—a derogatory term that over-identifies the children with what they *do* rather than who they *are*—the small children were digging through garbage looking for anything they could eat.

When they were very young, their father had abandoned them. Their young mother began scavenging through dumps and trash heaps looking for things that could be salvaged and recycled. She would sell the scraps that she found, but it wasn't enough to provide for her family.

Around the world—in every country—some version of this dehumanizing way of survival mars the dignity of women and men, girls and boys, all who bear the divine imprint of God in their humanity.

A short time before our community met the children, a fire broke out in the slum where the family was living. Everything was lost. The children were found living on a train platform, begging, neglected and slowly starving to death. They were so malnourished that even the introduction of regular meals made them sick.

The irony of the collision of our community's lives and the lives of these little ones during the Christmas season is tucked into their names. The boy, six years old, is named Joseph. His four-year-old sister's name is Mary.

A mere two weeks before Christmas, the arrival of our young Mary and Joseph presented us with an opportunity to practice hospitality—the kind of hospitality that seeks to recognize the disguise of Christ in those who are poor and marginalized.

WHY LOCATE OURSELVES ON THE MARGINS AMONG THOSE WHO ARE POOR?

What compels us to develop relationships with those on the margins? What makes people willing to make themselves available like this? What are the implications of a spirituality that discovers Christ among the most vulnerable of the world's poor?

Over the years, our community has spent countless hours reviewing passage after passage of Scripture referring to the or-

phaned and widowed, the hungry and defenseless and the vulnerable and needy. Throughout Scripture we find a number of
generative and recurring themes that challenge our isolationist
mentalities regarding the needs around us.[1] Rather than reading
the passages out of context or reducing them to trite responses
of benevolence to be practiced by the nonpoor, we read the
Scripture and then ask the question "What does this say about
God's character or action on behalf of those on the margins?"
Reading and rereading Scripture in this way has not only opened
our minds to a depth of God's essence expressed in God's love;
it has softened our hearts as we allow ourselves to be embraced
by our friends who suffer.[2] Put simply, Christ makes it very clear
that all in need are our neighbors, many of them in fact our
brothers and sisters.

Poverty in the kingdom of humanity is a lie that dehumanizes
the very essence of humanity by marring identity and dignity.
Poverty in the kingdom of God releases and enables our identity
and dignity to be found in the slain Lamb. Poverty in the kingdom of humanity is offensive. Poverty in the kingdom of God is
redemptive. Poverty in the kingdom of humanity is imposed;
people who are poor do not choose their poverty, but it is forced
upon them. Poverty is embraced in the kingdom of God; Jesus
became poor that we might become rich.[3]

As Christians, we must find our true dignity and identity in
Jesus. Part of this process includes overcoming the false identities, such as those formed through our lusts for power, security
and self-importance, that hinder us from knowing God. Through
Christ and by renouncing our status and self-centeredness, we
can embrace our true identities as frail and interdependent. John
D. Zizioulas, a Greek Orthodox theologian, says our identity as

Christians is as persons in relationship with others.[4] Here the core of our identities is called into question. Our false identity says that we exist through autonomy, apart from others and even at the expense of others. But in God's kingdom, we are not to seek our own interests but the interests of others (Phil 2:4). Our identity becomes *ex-centric*—that is, our identities are transformed with and through others. And, by discovering our true identities, we also make ourselves available to secure justice by affirming the dignity and identity of those on the margins.

Jean Vanier, who has given his life to the mentally and physically disabled through the L'Arche communities, sums it up beautifully: "People may come to our communities because they want to serve the poor; they will only stay once they have discovered that they themselves are the poor. And then they discover something extraordinary: that Jesus came to bring the good news to *the poor*, not to those who *serve* the poor!"[5] Vanier teaches us that the broken ones are those who lead us to our brokenness and awaken us to our need of a healing Savior. In this way, the broken lead us to Jesus—to healing, wholeness and resurrection.

THE MEANING OF MARGINAL: LETTING THE MARGINS SUBVERT THE CENTERS

By affirming our commitment to those on the margins, we reveal our prejudgments and assumptions about the "center." The dominant culture attempts to define the social, economic and political "centers" and tries to dictate our values so as to direct our way of life. The voice of the dominant culture tells us how we should relate to one another, what we should own and how we should exert ourselves in the world. These centers are accepted to such an extent that they are seldom called into question.

It is not surprising that after becoming Christians, we begin to redefine our understanding of the world's centers. Yet this is often not radical enough. We may unwittingly find ourselves reaffirming the world's centers long after becoming Christians. Whereas we see the value of serving others and of relinquishing our power and possessions and living a just life, we may continue to esteem progress, pop culture, business agglomerations and unaccountable American democracy. While one could argue the benefits of these ideologies and entities, they largely remain unquestioned centers of the dominant culture.

When we accept the dominant culture's definitions, if we see someone who does not experience the so-called developed world's perception of these "higher" standards of life, we may pray that they would. Assuming our standard to be the best, we might pray for God to help a person get a job where she has the opportunity for advancement, but we might fail to consider the effects of the business on the rest of society. We might pray for a person to acquire nice clothes, a better car and other material things, but we might fail to question our tendency to always want more. We might pray for someone to get an education or technical training, but we might not question the ethics that are implied. We might pray for things that are relative to our own standard of living or a standard of living set by those who have more than us. Though benevolent, could these prayers be misguided?

While our desires for a better life may look good on the surface, there is an underside to each. Progress is defined by the powerful. The underside is that a minority consumes most of the world's resources in the name of modernization. Pop cultural imperialism imposes consumerism and narcissism on a global scale. The underside is that a minority consumes more than it can afford and that a majority loses its own cultural identities, cannot satisfy its inflated desires and must work grueling jobs of production to ensure that the minority gets an "affordable" product. Big business is championed as wealth-creating and peace-making. The underside is that multinational corporations exploit the vulnerable and powerless and are not held accountable for their actions. Western democracies perpetuate their reign over the globe with little critique. The underside is that less powerful governments allow more powerful governments to influence and manipulate the interests of their own people.

Samuel Kamaleson, former World Vision vice president at-large, says that we all have our two bits invested in Babylon. That is to say, it is against our own interest to point out the evil from which we benefit. So we must project the absence of evil, hide our inconsistencies and disguise our wickedness. By owning the benefits from the dominant culture, we accept the categories it uses to define good living, and we then impose these values onto others. Instead of seeking a critique of the dominant culture, we live by it. We accept corrupt values rather than suffering the loss of power, privilege and prestige. And we perpetuate the underside of our values by forcing others to live by them as well.

It is only when the church relinquishes the privileges of the world's power centers that we can denounce its tactics. It is only when we Christians detach ourselves from the world's claims on us that we can find the power to criticize its values. In fact, when we call these "centers" into question, we find ourselves marginalized. Yet, by holding up marginality as a value, we may unwittingly validate the centers. Instead, we must subvert the centers and redefine them.

THE "MARGINAL" NATURE OF GOD

Certainly, marginality is a biblical value. Not only does Jesus commission his disciples in every generation to take the gospel to the margins of the earth (Acts 1:8), he also calls us to the margins of society, to those who are poor and outcast (Mt 25:40). Not only does Jesus call the church to obey these commands, but he also models them for us. He is born into the world not in a palace for kings but in a village. Even in the village, there is "no room," so he is found among the animals in a barn. When Herod seeks the newborn king, Jesus is taken outside the country and becomes marginalized as a refugee. Most of Jesus' life is spent in obscurity in Galilee, marginal to the world's powers. In Jesus' public ministry, he spends most of his time among the marginalized multitudes.[6] When Jesus does confront the centers of power, they react by marginalizing him. Ultimately, he is excluded from life with us by being taken outside the camp and crucified (Heb 13:12).

The mandate for the margins is not simply a strategy to get the gospel out to the whole world; rather, the movement toward the margins is primarily a reflection of God's heart for the world. When we walk with God, we are directed toward the margins because this is the way God works in the world. And when we see God on the margins, we find that what the world calls marginal is central for the church.

The new friars seek to serve Jesus among the most vulnerable of the world's poor. At times this is overwhelming and may feel depressing and isolating. We often feel that we are without answers, without hope and alone. Among our friends who are poor, we are surrounded by hunger, abuse, violence, suffering and death. Exactly where we intended to minister to Jesus, we often sense his absence. Confused and distraught, we come to utter the question that lingers tacitly in our souls: where is God?

Though we pray and pray for God to intervene so that an impoverished girl is protected from those who would exploit her, she still ends up in prostitution. Where is God? Though we try to assist children on the streets, many still make their homes in the sewers and on the sidewalks. Where is God? Though we pray for God to be the provision for and protection of the vulnerable ones, a little boy begging on the street corner is still run over and killed. Where is God?

In our despair and disillusionment, the response, though sometimes tarrying, comes as a surprise. Amid the social outcast and diseased, next to the abused and dying by the roadside, between the condemned sinners, Jesus is present. Precisely where it looks most godforsaken, Jesus is intimately near. Jesus so identifies with the marginalized that he promises his presence in the marginalized: "Just as you did it to one of the least of these who are members of my family, you did it to me" (Mt 25:40 NRSV). Sometimes we unwittingly anesthetize the sting of this promise. We think that the hungry, thirsty, naked and imprisoned Christ would be satisfied if we would just help him out a bit. It is not simply loving action that is demanded for the "least of these," however. In the first place, it is a call to faith.[7] Only by faith can we affirm God's presence where it appears God is absent. Just as we are called to hope against hope (Rom 4:18), we are called to faith against faith. In the suffering, dying and distress of the poor, we are confronted with all that does not correspond to our concepts about God: someone who is stricken, despised and from whom humans hide their faces. Precisely in the margins, where God seems wholly absent, we are called to faith in God's presence. By faith, we identify Jesus in the "least of these" and are compelled to respond in loving service.

In this way, the margins are not so much a location as an orientation. We may be in the Midwest of the United States, working for the well-being of immigrants, or in the almost uninhabitable regions of El Alto, Bolivia, building relationships with those trapped in exploitative jobs. We may be located in bustling London, amplifying the voices of the marginalized, or in the sewers of Romania, bringing food to children living or working on the streets. Indifferent to our geography, our energies and attention are directed toward Jesus' promised presence among those on the periphery. Thus, God is not so much calling those on the margins back to the center but is defining the margins as an alternative center.

ON THE MARGINS AMONG THE EXCLUDED

As Christians, we are reoriented toward the margins. But outside the world's centers, we find not only those who are marginalized from relationships, education, resources and other avenues of empowerment, but also those who are excluded. That is, they do not simply lack access and power; they are *denied* access and power.

We have friends in a slum in Sierra Leone called Kroo Bay. There the people suffer from malnutrition, disease, overcrowding and, during the rainy season, flooding. The government's response to the slum was not to invest in its development but rather to cover it up. A high wall was built to separate the slum from the main road. Out-of-sight meant out-of-mind; it was an act of intentional exclusion.

Kroo Bay is the poorest slum community in the capital city of the world's poorest country.[8] It is a former fishing village that has turned into an informal coastal slum with approximately six thousand residents, more than four thousand of whom are children.

Located below sea level, where two of Freetown's major rivers meet and flow into the Atlantic Ocean, Kroo Bay is flooded with sewage every time the city receives a major rainfall. This forces residents to spend countless days and nights fighting to save their homes, bucket by bucket. It's overcrowded, congested and clogged with trash. If it weren't for the laughter of the children and the smiles of the vendors, Kroo Bay would seem like one of the most hopeless places in the world.

It is said that there is only one proper toilet in the entire community, forcing many of Kroo Bay's residents to defecate in public. One-fourth of Kroo Bay's children will not live to see their fifth birthday, and a tenth of the families in the community have lost a loved one to sickness or disease (typically cholera or malaria) in the past month. Considering the major technological advances in the twenty-first century, combined with the billions of dollars spent on aid to Africa, it's hard to believe that there is really a place like this on earth.

Noah Tullay runs the Good News Club in Kroo Bay. The Good News Club is a weekly Bible study that includes joyful praise, dynamic Bible stories, heartfelt prayer, compassionate first aid and nutritious food. Noah grew up in the Kroo Bay community with his father's two surviving wives. He never knew his own mother. His dad died when he was ten years old. Having overcome seemingly insurmountable obstacles, Noah left Kroo Bay to complete his education. He then returned to the slum that was his childhood home.

His return is a sign of hope, an indictment against the plundered childhoods of Kroo Bay's little boys and girls. It reminds them to dream past the clutches of poverty on their own lives. His return stands as a prophetic statement against poverty's assault on the oppressed humanity of Kroo Bay—a deeply spiritual affirmation that every human being carries the image of God in her or his intrinsic beauty. Noah's return is a tangible sign that the kingdom of God has arrived in Kroo Bay—inviting us to follow him and our friends who are poor, because God is present there.

On our numerous visits, Noah has taken us to his modest home in the slum. We have sat in his front room as he offered us cold drinks. One day when we are visiting, we walk with Noah down the steep hill from his home to the floodplain, which fills with water and refuse during the rainy season. The further down the hill one goes, the poorer things seem to get. Eventually we arrive at an old, dilapidated church. With several broken windows and a tropical weather-beaten exterior, it is unbelievable that the building can still be used.

This church is where Noah conducts the Good News Club. Every week nearly three hundred children are ushered, quickly yet gently, into seven rows of old wooden pews. Once the pews are filled, kids stand against the walls and in the aisles.

Church happens there in a way we had never seen before. Our new friends David and Joseph begin the service, leading the few hundred children in song and dance. We are told that during the civil war, Joseph was conscripted by the rebels and forced to fight. As a child soldier, he was a victim himself; now, watching him lead the service, one would never guess that Joseph must have carried out unspeakable atrocities during the war. Beaming with joy, Joseph is one of Kroo Bay's many reminders of grace. His past is still being redeemed, and his life is being restored. Joseph's joy and enthusiasm are inspiring. The songs he sings are truly angelic. His praise to God is a prophetic utterance of hope realized.

Joseph, David and Noah have been joined by a few others who have made substantial sacrifices to serve Christ among the poor. Cami Sigler left a strong community and a stable job in southern California. Faye Yu put a high-paced life of influence in Washington, D.C., behind her. Stephanie McGuire grieves the loss of proximity to her loving family in a small midwestern town. All three obediently and faithfully set out to discover Jesus amid the suffering in Sierra Leone.

Once the singing concludes, Noah shares a simple reflection on Scripture and a challenge to find the goodness of God in a bad world. After church, the WMF staff members join David and Cami in setting up a makeshift first-aid stand. During our visit, we sit stunned as we watch child after child come forward to have painful boils or open wounds washed and bandaged and gruesome infections treated. We are shocked to see how suffering is the commonality shared by every child in that church.

We sometimes refer to Noah as "St. Noah of Kroo Bay," in memory of St. Francis of Assisi who was called to rebuild the church. What is it about Noah's life that is so inspiring? How is God using Noah in such compelling ways? Why has Noah chosen to remain on the margins when many other opportunities are in his reach?

Is it his prayerfulness? Is it a hope against hope, a lament for inequality and an affirmation of the dignity of his neighbors? Is it his commitment to poverty? Noah doesn't have to live in Kroo Bay, but he does. In fact, he came back to Kroo Bay after escaping its devastating grasp on his life. Even more, Noah has entertained the opportunity of leaving his home to study finance in England, yet he remains among his friends—the victims of poverty's relentless and oppressive prison.

Is it his vision and vocation for restoration? Noah believes in the potential of God to change the lives of the children with whom he worships. That is real church. That little, broken-down, poor excuse for a building at the bottom of the slum is the church. That is where God is.

It is in the Good News Club in Kroo Bay where the open wounds of Christ's body still bleed today. It is the testimony of Noah's life that tends to these bleeding wounds, ministering where the heart of God breaks today.

Reflecting on the lives of Noah and St. Francis, we find a number of marks that make for an effective commitment to establishing hope where there is suffering.

Building community on the margins. Given an exceptional calling, St. Francis and Noah threw themselves at the mercy of community. Journeying with a team is not only practically helpful; it is theologically central to the relevant expression of the love and presence of Christ among those who are poor. We have watched Cami's life and ministry take shape through her service with Noah. Cami's friendship with Noah has been an expression of mutual accountability, and it has supported and inspired their commitment to community.

Embracing poverty with those on the margins. Living a lifestyle that reflects respect for friends who are poor and those who suffer pressed Francis and Noah into an embrace of poverty and a celebration of simplicity. The invitation for Cami, Faye, Stephanie and others to experience community in Kroo Bay is a hinge to the privileged and affluent lives of those of us who come from the West to the lives of those suffering in slums. Noah has created an open door for the transformation of our community; taking part in the life of Kroo Bay's community gently challenges us to map the incarnation with our own lives.

Rebuilding the church at the margins. Finding a spirituality that sustains is one thing; thriving in the faith is a mark that characterizes St. Francis and Noah and the community that has given itself to the people of Kroo Bay. This spirituality roots itself in a contemplative posture before God and the formation of a serving community expressing itself through worship. Celebrating voluntary poverty creates freedom for ourselves and others; it is a new way of being and doing church.

Although many of us have visited this slum, most of us haven't stayed. As much as we may orient ourselves toward the margins, either by choice or consequence, we still maintain access to power and relationships. Hence, our movement toward the margins is limited. Still, our friends like Noah have grown up in Kroo Bay and, though they could have moved out, they have intentionally chosen to stay so as to witness to the inclusive kingdom of God among those excluded by the power centers.

This challenges us to take a bigger step. First, we need to recognize that much of today's church is, in fact, among the excluded.[9] Second, we need to submit our orientation toward the margins to the input and direction of those who have been excluded. They not only know how best to lead us to the margins, but they also have cultivated fellowships of spirituality that are not based on economies of surplus or political advantage but on the power of the gospel and the inbreaking kingdom of God.

In the last few months, members of our community in Romania have become friends with a group of about twenty refugees from the Congo. They left their families to work jobs that they contracted in Romania. After a few months of working long hours without receiving their promised pay, they were fired. Their families had expected provision while waiting in their war-torn home. Instead, their breadwinners are being exploited in Europe. They are not marginalized by choice or by the consequences of their decisions but by the inability to resist the powers imposed upon them. They are excluded. Still, one Congolese told us, "You need to learn how to worship. We worship until we are drenched in sweat. We worship for hours. In the midst of suffering, hunger and tribulation, we receive strength and encouragement from God through worship." This is where the marginalized get their power for life. It is here that the excluded church is leading and teaching us. And this is where we are invited to transformation by becoming a church of the excluded.

RESISTING THE PULL OF FALSE "CENTERS"

The dominant culture acts like a gravitational force, pulling us toward its values and ways of living. In Scripture, we find Elijah, whose prophetic stance from the margins teaches us tactics to resist the pull. When the Promised Land dries up because of recalcitrant rulers, the people suffer and die (1 Kings 17). Although all are affected, the vulnerable and those who are poor suffer first and the most. God tells Elijah to go to a nameless widow (1 Kings 17:9). Elijah requests her hospitality, and although she has nothing extra to give, she gives what she has. Ironically, it is through Elijah that God provides an unending supply of daily bread for the woman and her son (v. 16). God does through Elijah what the power centers have failed to do. In fact, when the widow's son later dies, it is Elijah who finds strength to pray for revived life in the middle of famine and death (v. 22).

But it would be a mistake to simply associate the miraculous revival of the boy with Elijah's prayer without taking into account Elijah's lifestyle. By denouncing the center's claims to power, Elijah has been marginalized. Rather than drinking from the king's provision, he has followed God, which has meant death threats, displacement and eating each day the regurgitated offerings of the ravens (v. 6). On the margins, Elijah stands on different ground, which gives him a different perspective. As theologian Walter Brueggemann says, Elijah's dining with the birds "is what gave him energy and courage and freedom and authority" in bringing faith and life to the widow and her son.[10]

THE MARGINS OF OUR COMMUNITIES

The orientation toward the margins is a task not only for us as individuals but also for our communities. In the early church, Christians were called *paroikoi*, from which we get the words "parish" and "parochial." In 1 Peter 2:11, Christians are described as being *paroikoi:* aliens who resist the powers of the world and who, because of their resistance, keep a distance from society's ideals, values, institutions and politics.[11] Also, in classical Greek, *paroikoi* means "the margins of the house." Christians understood themselves to be strangers in the world and, therefore, made their parish with those living on "the margins of the house." The family of God was active and attentive at the margins, among the hurting and those suffering from social, religious and economic exclusion. The social position of *paroikoi* became a new locus where those outside came to belong to community. In this way, the church was a community that created its center on the margins. The family of God existed as a home for the strangers and marginalized.

Contrary to worldly structures, the margin was not a dividing line that indicated who was in the family and who was not. Defining our collective identity by what we are against is called *parochialism*—the exact opposite of what the *paroikoi* meant and stood for. "The margins of the house" are not where we stake our ground and build our fences. When we do that, we act not like the kingdom of God but like the world, which sanctifies and guards its national borders. The church, rather, is always to be negotiating "the margins of the house" as a place where the exploited are healed, the lost are found and the excluded are integrated.

A mobile *paroikoi* is found on the streets of Lima, Peru. Since 1996, members of the WMF community in Lima have been going into the red-light areas to meet with young people who live and work on the streets there. Two or three nights a week the community members gather at a church where they make a hundred or so sandwiches and a large bucket of something hot to drink. Armed only with love and an acoustic guitar, they make their ways to an alleyway where many of the young people gather.

From 11:00 p.m. until the wee hours of the morning, a meager meal is shared, a few songs are sung together, and a prayer is uttered. All of this is plastered against the backdrop of dirty and dangerous streets. Typically, many of the youth and children carry around small cellophane bags of shoe glue or industrial-strength paint that they "smoke" (inhale by placing the bag to their mouth and nose to breathe in the fumes) to get high. It helps them feel less hungry and distracts them from the real pains of the hardships they face day in and day out.

The informal and often impromptu gatherings on the corner of that alley have become times of refuge, worship and peace for children whose lives are marked by violence, uncertainty and abject poverty.

Fernando, one of the youth on the streets, was approached by Danielle Speakman, a former WMF intern, who was doing research on the population living on the streets for her graduate program.[12] She asked Fernando if he goes to church. Danielle expected Fernando to say that he is not welcome in church, but instead he answered, "Yes." Surprised, she asked, "When do you go to church?" Fernando replied, "Each Tuesday and Thursday night when we meet with the community on the streets to worship and eat together."

Church happens not because of the intentions of the staff who gather there but because of the openness of the children and youth. It is their willingness that allows for an environment where God's presence is affirmed. They have taught us how to see church differently. We have learned to follow them to places of worship in the midst of suffering, places of celebration in the midst of sorrow and places of peace in the midst of violence.

ANTICIPATING THE END OF THE MARGINS

The church's active presence on the margins is informed by its hope and vision for the future, in which Jesus returns to renew the heavens and earth, to restore his kingdom in fullness and to bring those on the margins into his healing hands.

Sadly, when the church became a power-wielding institution, the original hopes for the future were co-opted. The institutional church's vision came to see the future as the continuation and extension of the church's power in the present and the establishment of the kingdom of God as the expansion of the church's reign. In contrast to the institutional church's vision, mendicant orders and monastic communities saw the future in radical discontinuity with the present reality, in which the church is a sign but not the realization of the kingdom.

While the institutional church's hope for the future legitimized its actions, claims and power in the present, the monastic and mendicant communities denounced that power, its claims and its legitimacy. Today, the institutional church believes in the continuation of the present. It seeks political, economic, social and even military might, believing that Christians are the best candidates to wield power in the interests of humanity and, ultimately, in the interests of God. The thought is that though the future may entail great calamity and destruction, the church's power in the present will be transferred to its power in the future. Therefore, the institutional church defends its power in the status quo. The new friars hold a different eschatology, however; like the mendicant and monastic orders, the new friars have an alternative view of the future. Signs of the kingdom of God are breaking into this world as a pledge and foretaste of its consummation, when God will renew all things. As new friars, the mendicant and monastic communities call the church to read and explain these signs but not to control them, because all power belongs to the Lamb. Because the kingdom of God subverts all other ultimate claims to power, the mendicant and monastic communities qualify and at times denounce other claims to and uses of power.

The church's waiting in the present is characterized by its hope for the future. The church is the messianic community that proclaims the Messiah, living under his anointing and anticipating his return (2 Cor 1:21). The church is also messianic in its hope and prayer. We pray, "Maranatha! Come Lord Jesus!" We look to the Messiah's coming for the complete liberation of humanity and creation, the true exodus from sin and torment and the real return from exile. The hope of the church is based on what God has already done in Jesus and what he has promised to do. We anticipate the future promises of God through our present experience.

The messianic community also anticipates the second coming by prophetically pointing to the "not yet." We articulate the heart of God and express the emotion of God for salvation, justice, holiness and renewal in the world. The church calls these things that are not as if they already were (Rom 4:17). This is the prophetic nature of the church.

Where does this lead us? Although the answer may be painful and difficult to accept, what are the natural implications of throwing ourselves at the mercy of friends in need and following them to the heart of God? What does it mean to submit ourselves to the salvific potential and sacramental nature of those who are poor?

From within the incubator of hope that was the first WMF

community in Chennai, India, we birthed two homes for children. One was a pediatric care home for girls and boys who are orphaned because of AIDS or who are actually HIV-positive themselves. The second was a home for children with profound mental and physical disabilities, called Samanthana Illam (literally, "The Home of Peace").

Samanthana Illam was, for many, a very difficult place to visit. The sounds could be overwhelming. Entering the doors of this home usually meant walking into a cacophony of cries, moans, grunts and sometimes screams. The children, all of them unable to speak, communicated in whatever ways they could.

The smells were often assaulting. Because the children were unable to speak, they couldn't express their needs—even the basic need of using the bathroom. So throughout the day the community members serving in the home were frequently required to mop urine (or worse) off the floors, bathe the children and then re-dress them.

The sights were at times unbearable. We found many of the children who were cared for in Samanthana Illam abandoned at government hospitals or on the sidewalks outside other childcare facilities in the city. In addition to their mental limitations, nearly all the children in the home were in one way or another physically malformed. This meant that most of the children couldn't even sit up on their own, let alone stand. Ensuring that they didn't develop bedsores was a constant task. There was even one precious child, Sheela, who needed to be restrained to protect her from repeatedly banging her head on the walls or floor. On more than one occasion, poor little Sheela had knocked her own teeth out; because of these violent episodes, she had several scars permanently visible covering her forehead.

Though sometimes seemingly full of chaos and pain, Saman-thana Illam really was one of the most peaceful places in our community. Visitors often commented on the presence of God experienced there and the nearness of God felt while interacting with the children. There really was something special about each of those children, and together they had somehow been able to negotiate their own form of community.

Two of the girls cared for there, Shanti and Fatima (also un-able to speak), were able-bodied and would freely move about the home with grace and gentleness. Joyfully they spent their days serving the other children. Sitting beside them, holding them, feeding them and in their own subtle ways attempting to translate what they understood the other children's needs to be, Shanti and Fatima were indispensable to the WMF com-munity members.

Despite their obvious limitations and needs, Shanti and Fa-tima were, in very real and tangible ways, leaders in that home and leaders for our staff members. In fact, the whole perceived power dynamics of that home were actually a reversal of what we would perceive as the norm. The collective group bore within them the nearness and presence of God in profoundly unique and palpable ways. Shanti and Fatima were a bridge to this divine group of angels, ushering the staff into the ability to serve Christ among the children by offering guidance and discernment of their unspoken needs. Our staff members were the ones transformed, finding themselves on the mar-gins of this worshiping community and having to learn and relearn what service meant from the children. They were typ-ically able to minister peace to the staff through their gentle-ness and love.

CONCLUSION

By orienting the church toward the margins, God leads us to
friendship and community in which our dignity and identity is
recovered and restored. By revealing God's self as marginal,
God subverts the world's claims to define the center and its
power over us. As the church affirms itself as the *paroikoi*, we
take our cues for identification and community with the so-
called marginalized from those who have been excluded. In
our action and presence on the margins, we affirm that, ultimately, only the power of the slain Lamb can transform the
world, and we anticipate that day. But God doesn't send the
church to the margins of the earth and of society just so that
people can be saved, community formed and the world transformed. God takes us to the margins so that the glory of God
may be revealed.

In Galaţi, Romania, we have developed drop-in centers and
community centers in order to develop community with children living on the streets. A few years back, our community in
Romania lost the lease on an apartment near the city center,
where many of the children with whom we were in relationship
worked, begged and lived. We spent a few months looking for a
new place, but it was difficult to find property and a neighborhood that was willing to receive marginalized and stigmatized
children. After exhausting the possibilities of real-estate agents
and want ads, we came to a forgotten neighborhood called "the
valley of the city." It was down the hill from the banks, universities and state buildings, in a wide flood plane. At that time, the
area was largely undeveloped and left to the risks and realities
of the flooding Danube River.

Many of the families of the children on the streets lived in this area, because land and rent were much cheaper if not altogether abandoned. We found a faded for-sale sign in the window of a dilapidated house, which we soon purchased and began renovating. When the time came to give a name to the community center, we called it what the kids and others in the city were already calling it: "In the Valley."

We named it not to reinforce the neighborhood's identity as being marginalized by the city, but as a place infused with Isaiah's prophetic promise: "Every valley shall be raised up, every mountain and hill made low" (Is 40:4). The centers are subverted and the margins are made central. Why? So that the glory of the Lord can be revealed and all people can see it together (v. 5).

Not only is the gospel taken to the ends of the earth to fill it with disciples. Not only is good news proclaimed to the lost and hurting at the margins of society. But the move to the margins is a participation in the infilling of the earth with the glory of the Lord.

New friar communities are situated in numerous places and spaces: in a home in Chennai with Mary and Joseph, in a slum neighborhood in Freetown, with a population of Congolese refugees in Eastern Europe, among a worshiping community of youth living and working on the streets of Lima, in a home for South Indian children with profound mental and physical disabilities and at the "In The Valley" community center in Galați. By discovering God on society's forgotten edges, those living in the so-called margins transform our perceptions of the centers. Here the centers and, consequently, the margins are being called into question and redefined.

Posturing ourselves on the margins, not as a location but an orientation, is an intentional act of devotion. It allows for a missional prayer to be offered through our submissive obedience. Together we bear witness to hope and live into an embodied answer to this prayer for *shalom*, transformation and authentic community.

6

Devotional

THE FOURTH SIGN

Phileena Heuertz and Darren Prince

Be still, and know that I am God.

—PSALM 46:10

"Martha, Martha," the Lord answered, "you are worried and upset about many things, but only one thing is needed. Mary has chosen what is better, and it will not be taken away from her."

—LUKE 10:41-42

Every year in San Francisco, InnerCHANGE inducts its new apprentices under the rafters of the oldest standing building in the city, named after its patron saint: Francis of Assisi. Mission San Francisco de Asis, now called Mission Dolores, was founded in 1776 by Spanish members of the Franciscan order. By welcoming our newest members in such a historical setting, we intentionally invoke a long-term, kingdom perspective among our members: God was at work here hundreds of years ago, and we are just a small chapter in the enduring legacy of God's unfolding story.

Participants are invariably struck by the hush of the cool interior stone, the intricacies of the Native American patterns on the painted ceiling and the ornate if not slightly rococo high altar. But eventually their eyes lock upon one of the most puzzling artifacts in the room: a protruding statue of a robed Franciscan friar carrying a cross in one hand and an extended sword in the other. Unfortunately, some of the early missionary fervor in California was mixed with the expansionist trappings of a land-grab for the king of Spain. This serves as a reminder to our incoming members that even in our zeal for expanding Christ's reign, our personal and cultural captivity can easily blind us to our motives and allegiances.

In short, those who have gone before us teach us by their righteousness as well as their sin. And before we rush to judge the stone friar, we must acknowledge how easily we are deceived as well, both by our sinful selves and the sin of our culture. It's true: we are shaped by what we're saturated in, which is why incarnation must always be paired with devotion.

For this movement of new incarnational workers, there's no denying the ways in which life in the slums and megacities affects us: the push and pull of overcrowded streets, the persistent smell of burning trash and the constant noise of honking cars, barking dogs and drunken fistfights spilling out into the roads. How do we pursue a life of intense, relational ministry in environments that are often as toxic as they are sacred? How do we forge a devotional stream that carries us deeper than our activist tendencies?

Thomas Keating, a Cistercian monk now in his eighties, says, "In the dark nights, consolations on the spiritual journey, including the rituals and practices that previously supported our faith and devotion, fail us."[1] This has been true for many of us serving among the world's poor. Many of us originate from white, middle-class families in the overdeveloped West. Our spirituality has been shaped by relative affluence and abundance of opportunity. Though it shocks some of our friends and relatives, we voluntarily embrace downward mobility to relocate among our impoverished neighbors. After a significant amount of time among our friends in poverty, we find that many of the prayers we used to pray, worship songs we used to sing and devotional reading we used to partake in no longer seem relevant.

A spirituality steeped in relative luxury and ease doesn't connect with our broken heart for our friend who sells her body because she has no other means to provide for her children. We find our faith wavers when we run into the same child at the marketplace day after day, a child who makes his bed on the street. And we often find it hard to worship with the lyrics we sang in suburbia when we remember that our neighbor is literally dying because he doesn't have enough food to eat. Daily facing injustice, violence and oppression challenges our faith and the practices that used to support it. We crave a deeper well to quench the thirst of our soul and that of our neighbor. We long to uncover a faith that transcends despair, pointing us to lasting hope while at the same time keeping us anchored in the harshest realities of human suffering.

For this movement of new friars to be both incarnational and devotional, we've needed to cultivate, often out of necessity, a truly sustaining way of life. In our early years, many of us discovered that neighborhood transformation was sometimes exhausting and seemingly never-ending. Ultimately, the hazards of our intentional incarnational presence led some to feel a lot less like the Samaritan fresh off the donkey and more like the half-dead guy on the side of the road. We had wounds that needed to be bandaged, and we desperately needed rest at the inn down the street!

Don't get us wrong: we don't mean to suggest we've tacked on *devotional* in order to make an already frantic life just a bit more bearable. Our members won't be sustained by a devotional practice that only exists to fuel more of our activist endeavors. No, in describing ourselves as devotional, we mean to say we've committed to a radical pursuit of intimacy with Jesus. Full stop. And in our communities around the world, this can be understood as an intricate dance of two unlikely dance partners: contemplation and action. Compelled by intimacy with Christ, we engage our neighbors and neighborhoods with enthusiasm and zeal, looking for the transformation that comes when Christ's kingdom is present. Likewise, with similar tenacity, and because the need for transformation in our neighborhoods is so great, we press toward intimacy with Jesus through individual and collective rhythms of prayer, Sabbath, silence and solitude. Without the riches delved in contemplation, we have nothing to give.

Mother Teresa, whose ministry among the poor is known the world over, has influenced and inspired many of us in the new friars movement both in her rich devotional life as well as her emulation of the incarnational life of Christ. Mother Teresa articulated the need for contemplation this way:

We need to find God, and He cannot be found in noise and restlessness. God is the friend of silence. See how nature—trees, flowers, grass—grows in silence; see the stars, the moon and the sun, how they move in silence. . . . We need silence to be able to touch souls.[2]

This kind of silence is more about an interior state than it is necessarily about external circumstances. Mother Teresa's Missionaries of Charity chapel faces one of the busiest streets in Kolkata, where it's rarely quiet. Nevertheless, the nuns who gather there still their minds, bodies and souls for regular, brief moments in their day—even amid the sounds of desperate people, blaring horns, diesel trucks and people selling their wares. Likewise, squarely in the field of service, throughout an active day at Nirmal Hriday ("House for the Dying"), every sister keeps to a routine of daily prayer. Amid a sea of dying men and women, at particular hours in the day you will find the sisters withdrawing from their work to pray in the upstairs chapel.

The Missionaries of Charity live a compelling devotional life. They observe a rigorous schedule of service accompanied by a regular period of thoughtful rest—one day a week; one week a month; one month per year; one year in every six. Mother Teresa, one of the greatest social activists the world will ever know, knew better than any of us that our labor on behalf of the poor is an expression of devotion to Christ. But she also understood the equal value of contemplation as a necessary component to authentic devotion.

Why does the contemplative dimension of life even matter? It matters partly because it sustains our members' sacrificial living. A deep, transcendent, abiding intimacy with Jesus is a well that never runs dry. But it also matters because our contemplative engagement with God can be good news for our neighbors and our neighborhoods. Could it be that practices like centering prayer and solitary retreats might realign our allegiances and prevent us from repeating the same colonialist mistakes of the past? Might our commitment to sabbath and theological reflection be valuable antidotes to the rampant consumerism and exploitation we find in Western culture, even within Western Christian culture?

The challenge for the modern movement of new friars is to build something as enduring as the Mission chapel in San Francisco or the ministry of the Missionaries of Charity—able to stand strong amid earthquakes, fires, disease and systemic poverty. Our challenge is also to build in a way that workers among the poor are not left immortalized in stone, swords in hand. Communities committed to devotion through both contemplation and action are postured to build such an enduring movement.

DEVOTION AS ACTION

Our technological advances keep us connected to a world in need. Because of Facebook, Twitter, BlackBerries and iPhones, we have no excuse to be unaware of the suffering of humanity. But while most Christians may only know the realities of the developing world through the media, our incarnational workers know them personally. Daily, we respond to the harsh realities of real children, women and men experiencing a living hell— abandoned to the streets, battling AIDS, eking out an existence in refugee camps or forced to sell their bodies. We encounter people of all ages trying to escape the horrors of poverty, war and exploitation. As people devoted to Christ, we are compelled to respond. So we go and we engage and we fight with all our might to turn the tides of inequality and oppression. We are driven by a vision for a better world, and we give our life to seeing that dream realized as an act of worship and devotion.

One hot, summer Kolkata night, I (Phileena) hurried with my teammates through the Howrah train station to catch transport to Mumbai. The weather in Kolkata at that time of year is sultry and steamy; there's no keeping dry and comfortable. I regretted bringing only one pair of cotton trousers—the green, hospital-scrubs kind—which had quickly become my most valued piece of clothing. How I wished I had at least one other option! The skirts I had brought didn't provide the comfort and ease of movement that my trousers did. I was so glad to be wearing the prized scrubs on this particular evening.

As I scurried with the team to find my train car and berth, I almost stumbled over an old, naked, dying man. Howrah train station is often filled with abandoned people who migrate into the city from their villages in the hopes of finding food or medical treatment. Not being able to speak the language, it was unclear to me what had brought the grandfatherly man to this terrible condition. Clearly he was dying; dying of hunger, thirst and most likely some kind of illness. Shockingly, no one stopped for him. Seeing that he was naked, vulnerable and crying out for help, I was compelled to stop. Knowing I had only minutes to catch my train, I quickly quenched the man's thirst from my water bottle, but proceeded on my way to keep up with the group. As I walked on, my mind was flooded with the words of Christ, "I needed clothes and you clothed me" (Mt 25:36).

Ashamedly attached to my one pair of scrubs, I contemplated the state of my soul and the state of the man in need. By the time

I reached the train car, I knew what I had to do. I slipped on one of my skirts and climbed out of my scrubs. With the green scrubs in hand, I darted back to find the man lying in his nakedness and vulnerability. With the help of my friend, I clothed him.

Through this kind of "devotion as action," we reflect Jesus, who engaged and confronted the ancient world socially, politically and religiously. By Christ's example we know that faith without works is dead, so we incarnate our faith in train stations, back alleys, sewers, brothels and slums. But more than *imitating* Christ, we *encounter* the Divine among our friends in poverty. As the Scriptures teach, God identifies with the poor and brokenhearted. What may seem like a life of sacrifice is really a hidden treasure for the worker among the poor. Relationship with marginalized people is an opportunity for tangible interaction with God. Something supernatural is occurring in our midst through acts of mercy and justice. Behold: action as an expression of our deepest devotion, opening the way for transformation around us and within us.

Several of the communities among the poor are inspired and renewed by the promises of Isaiah 58—that in our welcoming the stranger, clothing the naked and feeding the hungry, we will encounter the healing presence and divine guidance of God:

> If you spend yourselves in behalf of the hungry
>   and satisfy the needs of the oppressed,
> then your light will rise in the darkness,
>   and your night will become like the noonday.
>
> The LORD will guide you always;
>   he will satisfy your needs in a sun-scorched land

and will strengthen your frame.
You will be like a well-watered garden
    like a spring whose waters never fail. (Is 58:10-11)

Ours is a devotion fueled by the promises from Scripture that as we pursue justice, God's presence will heal, restore and guide us always. This is the divine intersection between activism and our best attempts at spiritual formation. Today's young Christians, especially in the West, have inherited a church that keeps mission and devotion at arm's length from one another. Mission is what you do for a summer before you settle down and get a real job, and devotion is what you do in private with your Bible and your prayer journal.

But Scriptures like Isaiah 58 show us a different way: a robust integration of active engagement met by the healing, guiding presence of Christ. As you feed the hungry and clothe the naked, "your healing will quickly appear . . . then you will call and the LORD will answer" (Is 58:8-9). In honesty, the life of active engagement fueled by intimacy demands more of us than wishlist prayers and formulaic devotional programs.

THE CHALLENGES OF ACTION AS DEVOTION

Activism is not unique to Christianity. Individuals of all faiths and no faith respond to people in need. Intimacy with Christ is what makes our action in the world unique—a very real, transcendent relationship between the God of the universe and us. We don't just pursue a life of mission on the margins because it makes the world a better place; anyone could do that. Rather, our activism becomes yet another expression of our deepest devotion. With intimacy as both our aim and our inspiration, the words of the great commandment become our creed: "'Love the Lord your God with all your heart and with all your soul and with all your strength and with all your mind'; and, 'love your neighbor as yourself'" (Lk 10:27). This isn't action for the sake of action but another form of our love relationship with the living God.

This kind of relationship requires both active engagement as well as quiet, still, focused attention—contemplation. God is encountered through both the active and contemplative dimensions of life; each dimension has its unique nature and quality. Knowing God in only one of these expressions lacks integrity, depth and fullness.

In the hurly burly of our modern era, activism tends to get more attention than contemplation. Just like anyone else, the new friars easily get caught up in our own busyness, frantically running from one crisis to the next in a cycle that looks less like loving the Messiah and more like trying to become one. Unfortunately, many of us in mission among the poor are so used to encountering Jesus in what Mother Teresa describes as "the distressing disguise of the poor" that it's easy to slip into a devotional style that could simply be activism cloaked in contemplative language. To put it another way, if we're not careful, some of us living and serving among the poor will camp out on the "distressing" part and never quite get to Jesus at all.

DEVOTION AS CONTEMPLATION

Activism without contemplation opens us to the risk of imposing our will on the world. If we are blind to our distorted compulsions, even our very best intentions and deeds can have selfish motives and exploitative effects. These hidden motivations

deceive us in the moment but are glaring in the rear-view mirror
of history—like the dark side of colonial and imperialist missionary endeavors. Without contemplation, we delude ourselves
into thinking we are above the sins of the friars before us. Being
enamored by our "good deeds," we can fall prey to seedy self-
righteousness and pompous piety. Activism needs to be held in
tension with contemplation to keep our devotion pure and di-
vinely motivated.

Our contemplative practices foster God-breathed perspective, allowing our motives and intentions to be checked. It allows me (Phileena) to reflect in the moment on my greed and
selfishness in the face of a dying, naked man, rather than re-
sponding from a place of smug self-righteousness. Contemplation nurtures a degree of transparency and vulnerability that we
are unlikely to pursue in any relationship other than with God.
In God alone we are safe to be our truest selves—the good, the
bad and the ugly. God is our Maker and knows us better than
we know ourselves. Though we may be able to hide from other
people by polishing ourselves as presentable and admirable, we
cannot hide from God. The contemplative life forces us to come
out from hiding.

Why is it that so many people resist being alone, still or quiet?
Solitary confinement is said to be one of the most dreadful of
tortures, yet people like Francis and Clare of Assisi, Ignatius of
Loyola and Mother Teresa of Kolkata knew their need for regular doses of it. We would be fools to presume we need anything
less. Some argue that temperament ("I just don't need as much
solitude as others") or culture ("My work ethic says it's good to
stay busy") allows us to neglect contemplation; yet such argu-
ments fall short in the face of some of the most diverse and ac-

tively engaged people to walk the earth. And it could be argued that a robust commitment to contemplation is the reason that the mission-order structures established by these heroes from history have endured.

We don't know how often Jesus withdrew from his active life to nurture devotion to the Father, but through Holy Scripture, we do know that he did. For example, just after baptism and just before starting public ministry, Jesus went into the solitude of the wilderness for forty days. Can you imagine? Some of us resist being alone for just *one* day!

During that period of intense solitude and withdrawal from the world, Jesus faced head-on the lies that all humans encounter in one way or another. Through the temptations toward power, possessions and prestige, Jesus had to dig deep within himself and honestly confront the lies: "I am what I do; I am what I have; I am what others say about me."[3] Jesus emerged from this period of solitude, silence and stillness knowing more fully who he was—the Beloved of God defined not by what he did, what he owned or what others said about him but by his relationship to the God-head.

Jesus was able to hear the voice of the One calling him, "Beloved." Christ's ability to hear and intentionality to listen allowed him to know how to serve. Jesus' rooted identity allowed him to know who to invest in, who to stop for and who not to stop for as he walked the streets.

Though Jesus was able to sift through these lies and illusions and reach the depth of his identity in forty days, the rest of us require entire lifetimes to live from such a place of truth. The lies that Jesus overcame in the wilderness are more likely to ravage and control us daily. How different might our days be if we could clear away the clutter, busyness and competing voices in our lives and hear the voice of God saying, "This is the way, walk in it"?

For this fellowship of incarnational workers, living in community and engaging real needs of desperate people can expose the lies in our exterior, active life and reveal our wounded and broken selves. But as we carry these wounds to Jesus, through a nurtured contemplative interior, transformation occurs. In God alone we find our identity, and nurturing a life of solitude, silence and stillness helps us to stay rooted in the truth of that identity.

Community life and relationships with our friends in poverty also reveal the inadequacies of our human response to the cries and desperation of our friends. God alone is supreme and all-powerful; our response and engagement is insufficient and inadequate apart from the life of Christ flowing through us.

Being honest about our need for the life of Christ within us is really the essence of embracing contemplation. Through contemplative prayer, we affirm that God is God and we are not, and that we are in fact desperate for God. Through contemplation we acknowledge that even our best good deeds pale in comparison to the life of God inspiring us and flowing through us. One good action exercised under divine inspiration has more power and effect than a thousand lesser deeds imposed on the world through our distorted and deceived motivations.

When we make regular time to withdraw from our active lives of service, steeping ourselves in contemplative practices like solitude, silence and stillness, we are forced to face our demons. By way of the intimate light of Christ, the dark (or false) side of our self is forced to come out of hiding and face reckoning. Through contemplation we realize with greater clarity that the toxic-sacred dual reality of our environment is also found within us. Through activism we confront the toxicity in our world, and through contemplation we confront the toxicity in ourselves. This is where our most desperate need for Jesus is realized, where the transformation of Christ can take root, molding us and shaping us into Christlikeness. In this manner, the reign of Christ in our neighborhoods is within reach.

Keating names the three temptations Jesus faced in the desert—power, possessions and prestige—as the basic "programs for happiness" to which all humans are vulnerable: power and control, security and survival, affection and esteem.[4] Whichever sin or program for happiness we gravitate toward will be the "demon" that rears its head to distort our activism. And without a commitment to contemplation, we are less likely to recognize that demon within us. Contemplation is the space and presence-of-being that allows for the dismantling of our demonic illusions. Abandoning and surrendering to the real presence of God around and within us allows for greater enlightenment of our true and false self. Contemplative practices reinforce a posture of constant abandonment and surrender to God—in our exterior as well as interior life. Devotion of this nature makes us supple in the hands of God. By way of Christ's dismantling work in us, we are liberated to love and serve more freely, purely and unconditionally—like Jesus.

Rather than divorce the active life from the contemplative life—as if it's reasonable to choose to live one way or another—an authentic and relevant devotional life brings balance or union to the active and contemplative dimensions. If we consider the wheel as a symbol for life or mission, contemplation will be found in the center axis, and the active or missional life will extend out in the spokes.[5] All the while the wheel is turning, progressing forward. Without the center axis, the spokes would lose their anchor and be unable to support the forward motion of the wheel. Without the spokes, the center axis would be deemed extraneous. When we are least connected to our contemplative center, our life is most tense and chaotic. When devotion is anchored in contemplative spirituality, the active, exterior expression of devotion is more peaceful, purposeful and effective.

THE CHALLENGES OF CONTEMPLATION AS DEVOTION

This kind of devotion—action and contemplation in union with one another—is hard. Our modern era, with advanced technologies and global awareness, exponentially speeds up the pace of life. Devotion that allows for stillness, silence and solitude requires us to slow down, shifting our gears from frantic down to fundamentals. How do our members around the world make time and space for this kind of devotion and intimacy with God in the midst of the pressing needs of the poor all around them? In short, the challenge must be met with creativity and commitment.

Some of our members have to regularly shut themselves off from the noise of the slums entirely, finding empty churches in nearby neighborhoods or silent retreat centers on the outskirts of town. Others consent to contemplation with the screeching brakes of traffic in the background, or with crowds of neighborhood children pressing their noses to the windows. One Inner-CHANGE member was known to escape to the confines of his beat-up Honda Civic for regular intervals of silence and solitude. (The car was humorously called "the chapel" until it was replaced with a fifteen-passenger van, which came to be known affectionately as "the cathedral.") Sometimes all we can do is light a candle or begin the day with a deep breath before diving headlong into the craziness. Devotional practice doesn't come easily in a context with constant demands competing for our attention. It seems our humanity is hardwired by our "programs for happiness" so that we too easily give into the frenzy that feeds our false self. It takes sincere creativity and commitment to live a truly devotional life. And herein lies the dirty little secret all too familiar to our friar-like members around the world: it isn't really our exterior context that distracts us from the devotional life.

Sure, we can blame it on the chickens or the children, the night club downstairs or the neighbors next door. But if you really press us, we'll admit it: we're just as busy as our growth-equity banker and lawyer friends back home, justifying our frenetic life in the name of doing ministry. It's our interior, not our exterior, that extends the greatest obstacles when fighting for contemplative space. And it is easy to want to avoid this challenge. Why? Because contemplative intimacy with God is completely countercultural and counter to our sinful nature as humans. In the contemplative life we are invited to face up to these lies: "We are what we do, what we have and what others say about us." Our personal, cultural and religious illusions are dismantled. We are invited to see ourselves for who we truly are—something that is excruciatingly difficult for us. It feels easier to live with the illusions we've created about ourselves, God and the world. So we resist. Change and transformation are hard and often painful, but an authentic life of devotion demands nothing less.

In Luke 14, we find Jesus eating at a Pharisee's house. As the meal goes on, Jesus tells a story of a man preparing a great banquet. In the parable, the master of the house invites many guests, but all of them decline the invitation and make excuses for why they can't attend. So the master demands that people of poverty and disabilities be invited. Not one of them refuses the invitation. One by one they come, and the master's house is filled.

The lesson is obvious. The excuses are plentiful, but those who are truly aware of their hunger respond to the invitation to commune with Christ, finding refuge and fulfillment at the feast of God.

Genuine devotion helps us recognize our need and deal with the pain in our hearts, common to the human condition. When we do, our community table becomes a more common place where inequalities between people of wealth and people of poverty are equalized. And our contemplative practice helps us more easily recognize that we are all essentially the same—naked, vulnerable people apart from the life of Christ.

Not only does a devotional lifestyle help rich and poor alike to recognize their desperate dependence on God, but intentional contemplation slows us down, fosters gentleness and patience and dismantles our false illusions of self, be they messianic or misaligned. Mariah Nix, a member working among the homeless of San Francisco, once compared the devotional life of an incarnational worker to her recent efforts at urban blackberry foraging. She captured some of her reflections in her journal afterward:

> There is pain in the search. As I picked, I became quite tangled in branches, reaching precariously for a beautifully ripe berry, while thorns attacked my hands and stuck

to my clothes. Yet it's worth it. The jab in the side or tangle in the hair was a cost I willingly counted for the sake of tasty fruit. So too with our search for the people God loves on these streets.

Sometimes it seemed the berries actually wanted to be left alone, huddled purposefully behind the protective covering of thorns. To pick them is a task that takes much gentleness. Recklessness only produces a scraped bloody hand and smashed fruit, but gentleness finds its way through the prickly parts until your fingers touch a soft piece of fruit that willingly falls into your hand. "Lord, make me gentle," I prayed. . . .

I began to tire and get a bit thirsty and kept telling myself it was about time to stop, but blackberry picking becomes addictive. Just when you try to stop a clump of ripe berries catches your eye from just beyond your reach. You must just go grab it . . . only to have another clump call from even farther. Before I knew it, I had traveled very deep into the middle of the bushes, into places I hadn't planned on going, moving one thorny branch to the side at a time. I was now surrounded by thorns and holding a big dripping bag of fruit in my hands. Love's pursuit of people leads step by step to places we never planned on going . . . places that if you stand back and look seem far too scary or dangerous to attempt. But if it's one thorn at a time, spurred on by the promise of treasure, we end up experiencing God's light in what appears to be the heart of darkness.

At last my bag of berries began to break, itself attacked by thorns, as if the bushes were trying to take back the fruit I had stolen, and I knew I had to stop before I lost

them all. I looked at all the unpicked berries still on the
bush and then down at the heavy bag dripping bright red
juice on my shoes, and I turned for home. Tomorrow would
be another day. This was God's table he had prepared. I
could return, but for now I had to leave. And so at the close
of each day we must rest in God as the one who pursues
and preserves us all. There is only so much I can do as his
servant in one day, one week, one year, or one lifetime.
There were hundreds of berries I did not pick that day. But
not a single one that he did not see. As I clambered out of
the bushes, another urban forager approached, bucket in
hand, in pursuit of berries with which to make jam.
"Happy berrying!" she hollered as she passed. I laughed.
Isn't this what the kingdom of God is like? Here I think I'm
the only berry picker, only to be reminded that others have
discovered the secret as well.

I stopped on the way home to capture my reflections in
my journal . . . staining its pages pink with messy fingers
. . . and I thought, "So it should be." The pages of our journals should be stained as we intercede messily for those
whom God loves.

A balanced life of devotion is hard because we've been raised
in a society of instant gratification, productivity and results. But
life and service among the world's poor often leaves us feeling
like there is very little "fruit" to point to at the end of the day.
Our incarnational communities around the world find that life
in the margins requires slow, patient, active work. Contemplation helps us to faithfully live into our calling in a way that sustains us for the long haul.

In addition, this kind of healthy contemplation-in-action is hard because many of us are commitment-phobic. We have a world of opportunity before us, crying out for us to respond, but we don't know who we are. So we go from one thing to the next in the hopes of self-discovery, unaware that finding ourselves usually comes in being still and genuinely connected to enduring community. Here, it's helpful to go back to the words of Isaiah 58. Not only are the promises of healing, redemption and guidance offered in our toil for justice; we are also reminded that real intimacy with God can be discovered in contemplative practices like keeping the Sabbath:

> If you keep your feet from breaking the Sabbath
>   and from doing as you please on my holy day,
> if you call the Sabbath a delight
>   and the LORD's holy day honorable,
> and if you honor it by not going your own way
>   and not doing as you please or speaking idle words,
> then you will find your joy in the LORD. (Is 58:13-14)

How interesting, isn't it, that the very passage that calls us toward a personal, hands-on response to injustice also beckons us to find the joy of God in our Sabbath rest as well.

DEVOTION'S MANY FORMS

Henri Nouwen aptly describes the necessary elements of contemplation and action in the devoted life. He writes,

> Prayer and action, therefore, can never be seen as contradictory or mutually exclusive. Prayer without action grows into powerless pietism, and action without prayer degenerates into questionable manipulation. If prayer leads us into

a deeper unity with the compassionate Christ, it will always give rise to concrete acts of service. And if concrete acts of service do indeed lead us to a deeper solidarity with the poor, the hungry, the sick, the dying, and the oppressed, they will always give rise to prayer. In prayer we meet Christ, and in him all human suffering. In service we meet people, and in them the suffering Christ.[6]

Whether actively pursuing kingdom justice or discovering the hidden joys of contemplative rest, our aim is to intentionally follow the winds of the Holy Spirit wherever they lead us. Ours is a calling to the gospel in its fullest dimensions: faithfulness in word, fidelity in our deeds and infused with Holy Spirit power. So we breathe in the Holy Spirit in our still moments of contemplative prayer. But we also encounter movements of the Spirit in our collective gatherings: words of wisdom, prophetic utterances, Spirit-led group discernment and faith-filled prayer for healing.

In many of our contexts around the world, the spirit world is alive and ever-present; disengagement with the evil spiritual forces preying upon us and our neighbors is not an option. Many of us have been blessed to learn the ways of the Spirit from our neighbors, incorporating greater openness and sensitivity to manifestations of the Holy Spirit into our prayer and worship gatherings. What a gift this is from our brothers and sisters in the Christian South and East, back toward the North and West.

In each of our communities, some of us are bent more toward activism and some more toward contemplation. As we journey together, however, we learn that the two need to be held in tension. While all kinds of worship and prayer styles, spiritual temperaments and Christian traditions are represented among us, growing in contemplation is something all traditions and temperaments can embrace at varying degrees and in different expressions.

So what does this look like for us as a daily reality? Every context is different, and each part of this global incarnational movement expresses devotion in keeping with its unique calling and contribution. For example, devotion is commonly encouraged through timely rhythms of service, prayer and fasting. In the Word Made Flesh (WMF) U.S. office that exists to serve and support its global community, many of the staff daily detach from their very demanding work to rest and pause at 3:00 p.m. to surrender to God through twenty minutes of centering prayer. Servant Partners members fast and pray for one another on the first Monday of every month, often pausing to contemplate Scripture throughout the day.

In addition, WMF founded the Community Care Center to bring broad, organizational attention to the rhythms of contemplation and action. Others open the door for contemplation through regular, actively engaged worship and praise. Several of the new friars organizations encourage members to set aside every seventh year of service for a sabbatical season of renewal, rest and reflection. Regular retreats away for solitude and silence are written into on-site schedules. Some weekly gatherings are infused with prayer and shared readings of Scripture in the *lectio divina* style.[7] Many in our communities pursue regular spiritual direction or have explored the spiritual exercises of Ignatius.

There are as many different contemplative practices as there are personality and spirituality types. Some of our members respond well to regularly kept Sabbath rest, others by a hike in the mountains or a visit to botanical gardens. The key isn't necessarily to impose one kind of devotional practice on our members but to encourage forms that forge a devotional stream that flows deeper and broader than activism alone. The goal, again, is intimacy with Jesus.

By way of conclusion, allow us to sketch a scene for you:

It is early Tuesday morning—another moment in a weekly rhythm when InnerCHANGE members, no matter where they are, pause to pray for one another. After numerous years of intercessory prayer meetings dominated by the pressing needs of our neighbors, we decided to confront our activist tendencies and allow space just to pray for each other as order members. Quietly, in living rooms and ad hoc chapels around the globe, we gather where we are able and pause for an hour to lift the needs of our community before the throne.

As we pray, we gather around a common set of symbols that serve as visual reminders from each of our locations, tokens of our connectedness: a cross from Romania, a cup from Guatemala, a photo of graffiti art in Los Angeles, a ceramic bowl from South Africa. Some teams light a candle and wait in silence. Others begin with singing. Some teams follow a centuries-old prayer liturgy, while others make space for the Spirit to write the script.

Tuesday prayer is often paired with a weekly time for members to reflect together on their previous week. Slowly meditating our way through the Gospel of Luke, or the book of Acts, we gather each week to savor how our Scripture reading and experiences of the week have come together into a common word God might be speaking. A candle is lit. A prayer or a song is offered. Then, often opening our journals, we share with one another.

Our Learning Community gatherings are at their best when each of our members has paused throughout the week to rest in contemplative silence. For some, this has meant getting out of the neighborhood for a long walk alone. Others have had to rise early or stay up late after putting children to bed. Some members have been away on a silent retreat, while others have been in the thick of active ministry, struggling to pull away at all. But each of us gathers our reflections from the week, and our journals become like jars of manna brought to share with the rest of the community. It is a sacred time, a holy pause in our week in which the Divine Author delights in threading our stories together.

This is the patchwork quilt of our collective contemplation: shading us during the "heat" of ministry and warming us during the cold seasons of doubt and discouragement. More than any off-site retreat for strategic planning or any vision-setting day with pie charts and expense reports, these humble gatherings are the place where contemplation and action come together in community. A place where we say, "Amen" to what God is doing in us and through us and where we plead, "Come, Lord Jesus" to the broken and barren places in ourselves and our communities.

What would it be like for our societies—even our churches—to quiet our frantic frenzy down to a whisper? Imagine the impact of a church whose activism flowed from a life of devotion rooted in contemplation. The new friars working among the poor aren't doing it perfectly, and we have plenty to learn from those who have paved the road before us. But our hope is to see poor communities transformed by the presence of Jesus: our feet planted firmly on the ground, our hands joined together in solidarity with our neighbors and our hearts ablaze with fire from the crucible of contemplation.

Communal

THE FIFTH SIGN

José Peñate-Aceves and John Hayes

If you have come to help me, you are wasting your time. But if you have come because your liberation is bound up with mine, then let us work together.

—ATTRIBUTED TO AUSTRALIAN ABORIGINAL ACTIVIST
LILA WATSON

At the end of my third year in InnerCHANGE, I (José) decided to take my three-month discernment in silent retreat at a monastery. In InnerCHANGE, we end our novitiate (years two and three) with a discernment period to reflect on our experience in the mission of InnerCHANGE and to listen to the voice of God about the journey forward. I discovered a quality of intimacy with God there in the stillness. One day, as I was meditating on the encounter of Thomas and the risen Lord, I was emboldened to ask, "Jesus, show me your wounds, that I might increase my faith." I had gone purposefully to the central chapel, and suddenly the faces of the gang members I was working with in San Francisco, many of whom had become friends, passed through my mind in a sequence. It was such a powerful experience I instinctively began speaking out their names—their very personal nicknames—like Shadow, Lazy, Cry, Solito.

As I surveyed their faces, I was overcome with deep sadness and began to cry bitterly. It seemed that in pressing my hands into Jesus' palms and side, I had been directed to trace my friends' faces and touch the deep wounds of our society. The streets of the Mission District, for all their unique beauty, spill over with poverty, drug and alcohol addiction, gangs, violence and relational infidelity. I sensed God reminding me never to be embarrassed about his wounds, but instead to embrace them and to embrace the people suffering those wounds. Only by living in true community with the people of the Mission, without shame, could I press my hands into Jesus' wounds and authentically feel their suffering. This was something I could not do alone, but had to do with brothers and sisters in missional community.

When I returned to San Francisco from my retreat, I shared with my team leaders that I wanted to step further into a calling to serve Christ among people in poverty with the InnerCHANGE community.

InnerCHANGE was not my first powerful experience of community. Like a lot of our members, I brought previous experiences of community with me; those experiences, in turn, have shaped me and have shaped our collective expression.

I am one of the few of my community's leaders who survived the persecution in El Salvador. I lost my pastors, my spiritual directors—everyone, it seemed. El Salvador is the smallest country in Central America, but it became one of the largest crucibles of suffering as students, labor unionists, *campesinos* and church members poured out into the streets to cry for justice against the oppressive leadership of our country. Those cries not only fell on deaf ears, but they were met with force: clubs, bullets, death squads and disappearances. The suffering and struggles of our people in El Salvador led us into one of the bloodiest civil wars in all of Latin American history.

In 1978, when I was just fourteen, I joined *Comunidades Eclesiales de Base* (Christian Base Communities). We were shepherded with gentle power by a nun named Silvia Maribel Arriola. We lived in a poor and marginalized working-class neighborhood of San Salvador.

We were young people in the base community, but ours was no ordinary youth group. Sister Silvia came to our neighborhood humbly, without pretense. She dressed like one of us, listened to us and ate with us in our homes. Consequently, we came to call her Madre Silvia. She gathered us into a community in which we could learn to celebrate the presence of the living God among us. Every meeting we would read a Bible passage and Madre Silvia would ask, "What do you think about it?" And then she'd continue, "How do you see this passage reflected in our neighborhood and in ourselves?" She was connecting the reality of God's story in the Gospels to the reality of our stories in our neighborhood. She was inviting us to look, analyze and act in the light of God's concern and compassion for us and those around us.

This understanding of the gospel demands that we must first transform ourselves. I learned that when a community is illuminated by the gospel and is committed to battling injustice and working for kingdom transformation, each member must move beyond his or her comfort zone and confront the needs and failings within. During this time, I heard Archbishop Oscar Romero, who was eventually martyred for his efforts to bring kingdom justice for the people of El Salvador, constantly repeat the phrase, "Hombres nuevos para una sociedad nueva" (loosely translated, "Men and women must renew their innermost beings to transform their society").

Archbishop Romero was a great light and a sign of what happens when the privileged are converted by the poor. He was a true leader, walking in solidarity with us, sharing our struggles and encouraging our hopes. Sunday after Sunday, Archbishop Romero announced the gospel but also denounced specific acts of injustice, demanded the release of the disappeared by name and called for a true and lasting peace.

In the excitement and inspiration of these times, our small base community invited other communities and other neighborhoods to join us. Little by little, we discovered that united we could do many things. We were able to organize around common needs to transform the neighborhood—to pave the street, to bring in electricity. Soon we were able to lift our eyes beyond our streets and glimpse the whole society of El Salvador with new sight.

But eventually our efforts to bring transformation were too threatening to escape the notice of leaders in a dictatorial government. On January 17, 1981, the people in power struck back. There was a massacre in our community in which ninety-three people were killed, including Madre Silvia. Her body was so badly burned no one could identify her.

In the wake of losing our leaders, many of us from the youth group responded to our profound grief by taking up arms. As a young man of sixteen, I joined the guerrilla movement. Eventually I rose to the level of a commander, and for ten years I fought with brothers and sisters for a vision of a transformed society in El Salvador. This season was my second powerful experience in community, and ironically, in some ways it reinforced qualities of community I had gained in the base community movement. We were not paid as guerrilla fighters. I fought side by side with volunteers who knew the cost of self-sacrifice. The intimacy and commitment we expressed to one another reflected relational patterns in the body of Christ. And as in my small base community, we acted and reflected in order to confront the forces against us. I have come to see that there is power in kingdom principles even when they are not used single-mindedly in the service of God.

After ten years of desperate combat in the mountains, I was tired, sick and disillusioned. I found myself no longer able to pursue the means and motives of the Salvadoran revolution, and I immigrated to the United States. That journey, largely on foot, required three attempts and took a total of seven months.

In San Francisco I met Nate and Jenny Bacon of Inner-CHANGE. Their humility and passion for the marginalized reminded me of Madre Silvia. In time, as I gradually surrendered to God, he began to renew in me the early roots of my faith. Together with the Bacons, we formed a mission outreach in the Mission District of San Francisco that especially targeted young men and women at risk, including gang members and ex-offenders. In a careful process of listening to, identifying with and suffering alongside, we were able to grow into a community. The people themselves developed and named our fellowship Communidad San Dimas. It is amazing how God brings so many things full circle. I sometimes say that now I have joined the real revolution—the one that is upside-down—working in community with and on behalf of the poor.

My experience taught me valuable lessons I have been encouraged to bring into InnerCHANGE. I learned that a community that brings renewal rests on renewal of self. And I learned that community must be knitted together in the power of God's love, and that love involves laying down one's life, not only after the model of the martyrs but in a daily renunciation of individualism and self-gain. In the war I experienced the power of a "band of brothers" pursuing a powerful cause. Vision is essential for communities to thrive—not just a vision to launch a team, but vision as an abiding presence that nurtures and inspires.

In experiencing the loss of Madre Silvia, I also learned that communities must be led in order to thrive. That leadership must be servant leadership and be in solidarity with those on the mission team and among the people served. As a man under authority and a man who exercises authority, I question some of the consensus models of leadership, in which everyone leads, that idealistic young missionaries sometimes adopt. These models can mask motives of reluctance to lead and reluctance to follow and can be out of step culturally with the majority world, which is typically more hierarchical.

POINT OF VIEW: BETTER TOGETHER

Incarnational, missional, marginal and devotional—taken together, these signs amount to heady wine and require an appropriate wineskin. It is challenging to wrap these powerful currents into cohesive community. But without careful attention to the wineskin, the new wine spills onto the ground.

As new friars, we have not discovered the elusive "perfect" community. There are no more perfect communities than there are perfect Christians. We want to be clear about that up front. In many ways, our models of communities in the sites in which we serve are works in progress. Still, the journey in community has been rewarding.

We (José Peñate-Aceves and John Hayes) are two members of the InnerCHANGE order, and we come to community from very different backgrounds. In one form or other, I (José) have been pursuing community nearly all of my life, from base community to guerrilla faction to missional order. The strength of those experiences has allowed God to use me with authenticity and credibility to gangs, which are fierce and often unyielding in their formation as communities.

On the other hand, I (John) am a North American who was born in the 1950s and came of age in the 1960s. I was shaped by both that epoch's inspiration and extreme individualism and, consequently, come to community with a natural instinct to elude it. I grew up in a family with middle-class values and aspirations but with a lower-class income, so there was much pressure to excel. A scholarship education in the Ivy League simply sharpened that drive for individual achievement. So it is with some irony that God used me to found not only a community but a fresh expression of order.

Together we represent a larger community, a "people" that is part mission, part tribe, part family. And beyond Inner-CHANGE, we are part of a wave of the Spirit raising up friars with fresh faces. We are modest in numbers, currently, but growing in depth and reach.

We write this chapter jointly because we have different points of view and together give a fuller picture of new friar community. Just as importantly, we write together because it is difficult to speak about community as an individual without distortion. Finally, our approach to writing has been to let two narratives drive the discussion. First, we have drawn insights from José's story, and second, we explore community from the vantage point of a story from Christ's ministry. Richard Rohr comments: "We do not think ourselves into new ways of living, but we live ourselves into new ways of thinking."[1] This has been our experience, and we have used the lived-in authenticity of story to convey that experience.

RECYCLING THE REVELATION OF THE WORD

In the early days of InnerCHANGE, we used to say that our inexperience caused us to "move into" the Gospels and then God shut the door behind us. Both Servant Partners and Inner-CHANGE are especially steeped in Luke, and we have choreographed much of our member formation to it. Our communities find life from all of the Gospels, however, and we find them foundational. There is vitality in Christ's ministry to people in the margins that is both inspiringly infallible and pitch-perfect practical. In feeding on the Gospels, we find ourselves continually "rising back to the bottom" in fresh cycles of revelation and service.

We have also found that, in diverse communities composed of many different nationalities, backgrounds and perspectives, letting the Gospel narratives speak can open dialogue in the space between us.

We are readers of the Word, but in practical terms, we also

posture ourselves to let the Word read *us*. We want the Word to read us in our own contexts and to become the hermeneutic for our lives. In that spirit, we'll turn to a passage in Luke.

AT THE GATE OF NAIN: A LOOK AT COMMUNITY

> Soon afterward he went to a town called Nain, and his disciples and a great crowd went with him. As he drew near to the gate of the town, behold, a man who had died was being carried out, the only son of his mother, and she was a widow, and a considerable crowd from the town was with her. And when the Lord saw her, he had compassion on her and said to her, "Do not weep." Then he came up and touched the bier, and the bearers stood still. And he said, "Young man, I say to you, arise." And the dead man sat up and began to speak, and Jesus gave him to his mother. Fear seized them all, and they glorified God, saying, "A great prophet has arisen among us!" and "God has visited his people!" And this report about him spread through the whole of Judea and all the surrounding country. (Lk 7:11-17 ESV)

All over the world, funerals like this one are taking place: a single mom burying an only son, mourners marching in rhythm toward an open grave. Sons should be burying their mothers, who lived to a ripe old age, rather than the other way around. But in a fallen world, in which Satan drives communities to desperation, mothers lose sons to knife crime in London, alcoholism in Caracas, drive-bys in Los Angeles and drug addiction in Nairobi.

There has been much fine writing on Christian community.

But less has been written that is grounded in the reality reflected in Christ's journey to Nain. In this passage, Jesus and his followers are not even in the gates of the city before they encounter a powerful need already spilling out the door. Community for our fellowship of incarnational workers among the poor must be rooted in this reality in which pain and need erupt in chaotic fashion. There is something about the words Luke uses—"Soon afterward," and then "behold"—that gives the same sense of vital urgency as the contexts in which new friars find themselves. This experience in Nain calls to mind knocks on the door in the dead of night, frantic calls from emergency wards that a son or daughter of the slum is dead or dying. Whether one is a remainer, a relocator or a returner, there is a random dynamic that goes with living in incarnational community in the slums and inner cities. Needs often catch us unprepared and are tailgated rapidly by others.

As full-time mission workers, we turn readily to the disciples in this story for our central model of community. The disciples are single-mindedly set apart to *go out* and minister with Jesus, and we identify with that. But this story in Luke depicts three intersecting communities. There are Jesus and the disciples, the crowd accompanying them in the journey to Nain and the community grieving in solidarity with the widow.

There are three insights from this story of Nain that are essential to our understanding of community in this fellowship of incarnational workers. First, Christ is at the center—not only of the redemptive activity at the gates of Nain, but also in the intersecting communities of disciples and townsfolk gathered here. He is the one who gives life and draws everyone into alignment; this alignment, in turn, brings kingdom cohesion and harmony.

Likewise, Jesus must be at the center of our communities.

Second, Christ ministers in community. He does not need the help of the disciples (or the accompanying crowd), but he chooses it. As contemporary disciples, we pay close attention to Christ's model and choose to minister in neighborhoods as collaborative teams. In fact, in InnerCHANGE we say, "It takes a community to reach a community."

Third, the disciples in Luke's narrative are alert to other communities playing redemptive roles in Nain. As new friars, we must be able to read beyond the disciples to appreciate the other communities identified in the text. Similarly, we must read beyond ourselves to embrace and value communities present in our context. The question "How can we be a better community of disciples?" is critical to us and is the question most Christian communities ask. But just as important is the question, "How can our community of disciples better fit into the story Jesus is writing in our neighborhoods?"

In this story from Luke, Jesus is at once the giver of life for the widow's son and the giver of identity for the overlapping communities. Identity is key here, because our human instinct in a fallen world is to define ourselves in ways that divide: this is "us," that is "them." There is no us or them in this passage, and that is a model for new friars. As highly committed communities that breed natural esprit de corps, we could reflexively read ourselves into this story as the disciples and not see beyond that posture.

But if we are committed to the integrity of community transformation and Christ's precedence in it, we will allow him to posture us in ways that are most empowering for the community in need. Sometimes we will be critical change agents, but sometimes we must be prepared to play a less celebrated role as members of the crowd. Sometimes we will be the mother, mourning a great loss. No matter what place we are given in the process of community transformation, we must appreciate all postures.

NATURE OF NAIN

Nain is a small village, twenty-five miles southwest of Capernaum and a long way from Jerusalem. This is the only time Nain is mentioned in the Bible. It is interesting that a place that could be so easily overlooked throughout Israel's history is found by Jesus. New friars are called to follow Jesus to marginal places like Nain: slums or inner cities, out of the way or shoved to the side, but with high levels of need spilling out the gate. Even when we deploy in major cities, we locate in communities that have been pushed to the periphery.

What does this have to do with community? Relocators and returners who have grown accustomed to viewing the world as a stage often find choosing Nain—telescoping oneself into a place and people on the margin—a very confining experience. With a backdrop of "bigger is better" that is promoted by the dominant culture, incarnation can feel like a mini-death experience: death to self-importance, death to the world's notions of leverage and impact. At times, mission strategists have suggested that in our willingness to live out the journey of the mustard seed, or grain of wheat, we're fixated on smallness.

This is why it is essential for our communities to keep alive a vision, particularly a vision of the upside-down kingdom. We remind ourselves that Christ's life was painfully local. Before his feet were nailed to the cross, Jesus chose to nail them to the ground in Palestine. And Palestine itself was a tiny backwater on the Roman map, a noisome pit bull in the side of the empire. We also find it helpful to refresh ourselves in parables like that of the shepherd who leaves the flock of ninety-nine to earnestly pursue the one lost sheep. In a sense, our communities must be prepared to concede the commonsense math of bigness to the enemy. Instead, we must cultivate allegiance to the power of the mustard seed.

Sergio Torres, a Latin American thinker, states that the first act of theology is commitment.[2] The fellowship of workers among the poor commits to communities like Nain. There is power for local people in that commitment. InnerCHANGE recently launched a new start in an off-the-radar township in South Africa. Soshanguve is not one of the more celebrated townships, and despite the fact that it holds more than a million people, no one from outside the township has ever moved in incarnationally to help empower Christian leaders. In the closing ceremony of a forty-day exploration in 2008 in which our staff and interns stayed with host families, our good friend and mentor Pastor Samson Mbonani explicitly noted how much the local community appreciated our choice to stay in the township. As he presided over the ceremony, he stated with great emotion, "We've had outside help before, but they always left at night."

We also commit to one another in our mission communities. All new friar communities explicitly covenant with one another in some form. In InnerCHANGE that covenant, or "rule of life," is expressed in seven commitments: humility, simplicity, purity, service, community, prayer and celebration. These commitments are both plumb line and encouragement for the journey together, and we refresh them by meditating regularly on them.

Committing intentionally to neighbors and teammates means downsizing our relational worlds. In the mainstream, with its illusion of unlimited relational possibilities, we can counter dissatisfaction in relationships by simply moving on in search of the "right people." But community on a mission team demands we cultivate friendships with people we might not choose ordinarily. Founding friendship on commitment rather than "chemistry" often requires adjustment for new members, especially single members accustomed to high levels of mobility. At the end of the day, however, we have found that any loss of chemistry in relationships is more than made up for with gains in meaning. That was the experience of Jesus' disciples, who left much to commit to Jesus' community. They did not choose one another but were chosen by Jesus. Yet they forged bonds that allowed them to transcend extreme adversity.

Finally, choosing to root our communal experience and identity in Nain and embracing its limits also means we must relinquish the goal of staying current—staying abreast of all that is going down in our postmodern, over-messaged world. In Nain, we will not be able to keep up with every sound bite on Twitter or random thought on Facebook. On the other hand, in committing to Nain, we discover the fulfillment of intimate relationships with flesh-and-blood neighbors and teammates in concrete place and time, and we escape the pressure of mainstream media to channel intimacy only as virtual embrace.

THE WEIGHTLESSNESS OF COMMUNAL SIMPLICITY

One of the things conspicuously absent in this story is the mention of "stuff." There is no record of Jesus taking anything with him in this story. Elsewhere we learn that Jesus often had a support team with him, largely made up of ministering women. But clearly, in this story they are not burdened with possessions. Certainly they are not dragging an RV behind them full of ministry props. We can take Jesus at his word when he says that "Foxes have holes, and birds of the air have nests, but the Son of Man has no place to lay his head" (Mt 8:20). Jesus and disciples traveled lightly.

Simplicity is a shared practice that we nurture as a fellowship of workers among the poor. It is an important commitment we make to one another as members, and just as important, a commitment we make to the host community in which we live and minister. As we suggested in chapter one, to choose Nain we have to live simply, not only to make more resources available but also to better identify with people in need we're hoping to reach—our neighbors and friends.

Simplicity, though, is more than a means to an end. It is a reminder that we must be less dependent on our possessions and that ministry in its elemental form is life on life. The apostle Paul declared: "But whatever was to my profit I now consider loss for the sake of Christ. What is more, I consider everything a loss compared to the surpassing greatness of knowing Christ Jesus my Lord, for whose sake I have lost all things. I consider them rubbish, that I may gain Christ" (Phil 3:7-8). Intimacy with Christ, as we experience him in our communal devotion, is often hindered by private ownership of many possessions.

Trying to manage a portfolio of possessions and positions *and* pursue Jesus and his abundance is a difficult—well-nigh impossible—task. We've found that simplicity liberates us for greater relational capacity for the communities to which we are committed: our mission community, our host community and the broader community of churches and other mission entities. Our commitment to simplicity as new friars is something we have in common with the historic orders; we have seen the fruit of that ancient wisdom in their lives, and their example has inspired us to persevere as well.

New friars are light in terms of possessions, but not necessarily light in terms of deeply held practices and symbols. Darren and Phileena have given us a sense of how symbol and liturgical practice create an abundance of meaning in our collective lives. But such symbols have more in common with the mobile ark of the covenant than with the stationary temple.

THE DISCIPLES AS LEARNING COMMUNITY

Our third insight from the story of Nain appears to spring out of the vacuum. We have seen how the smallness and seeming insignificance of Nain can be embraced, and how we need to travel lightly. But what's more, the disciples accompanying Jesus in this journey to Nain don't appear to be doing anything.

We contend that though the disciples are not active, they are nonetheless in a posture of active learning. How do we know this? We can infer this because the disciples do this kind of ministry, including the high-drama healing, on their own later on.

The disciples, even Peter, are speechless in this passage. So often we purport to be learning, but our mouths are moving. In the San Dimas Community, we are involved in some particularly sensitive ministry to young offenders in Juvenile Hall in San Francisco. The learning curve for new volunteers working with young people caught in gangs, drug dealing or drug abuse is high, and we ask people who are apprenticing with us to refrain from speaking on their first two visits with the team. We ask this not to quench their spirits but both to protect the privacy of the incarcerated young men and to protect the quality of the new team member's learning experience.

In the devotional chapter, we described the importance of being a learning community perpetually in formation. Bobby Clinton, professor at Fuller Theological Seminary and lifelong student of leaders, has found that the two things that contribute to leaders fulfilling their God-given callings are lifelong learning and community, preferably together.[3] This overarching perspective is important as learning can feel like drudgery, especially if language learning is involved. But to build in lifelong learning as a core community assumption gives our lives and ministry together added significance.

CHARACTER-CHISELING COMMUNITY

"Iron sharpening iron" is a visceral phrase that is active in practice, not passive. It entails speaking truth to one another in love, and demands that experienced members take time to model for those who are new. In the San Dimas community we liken this godly process to the sculpting of a bust. In the chiseling process, the uniqueness of our true face emerges, and yet, in the mystery of union with Christ, we come more and more to resemble him.

Most people come to community with higher expectations for it than aptitude to express it. Too often we are quicker with a prescription for others than a contribution. Practicing self-denial is one of the ways we put ourselves into the hands of God's chiseling community, and godly self-denial leads to self-discovery. In our communities, we've found we must be persistent but patient with one another, as lasting change often comes slowly. It takes time to trust the multiple eyes of community that illumine blind spots lying in the shadows of our egos. Often only in hindsight do the small workings of the chisel emerge as incremental revelations.

One of the counterintuitive lessons we've learned in community is that multicultural teams on the field often show more grace and manifest more precision in the sharpening process than teams of people from the same culture.[4] Diverse communities are often marked by a natural respect for and attention to observation. Same-culture communities, on the other hand, often exaggerate weaknesses and wear down to the lowest common denominator of the culture. A case in point: some of our early teams composed primarily of Westerners were plagued by the cultural weakness of individualism. Community in this case compounded individualism, and those teams dissolved or dispersed into individual ministries tied together superficially only by geography.

CONFRONTING ANTI-COMMUNITY

The enemy knows the power of community and knows Christ draws us inexorably toward it. He cannot eliminate it, since we are marked with the image of God, however clouded. That image, like the Trinity, draws us into community. But Satan can distort and disfigure community.

It is interesting how the enemy works to distort the power of community. In some cases he works to exaggerate community and in others to break it apart. Many of us have been working with gang members for quite some time. Gangs are communities in which Satan exaggerates certain community virtues into self-destructive levels of commitment and allegiance that bind members into powerful brotherhoods or sisterhoods. In contrast, in many churches and Christian communities, Satan often works extra-hard to ramp up the individualism, such that community means simply a seating arrangement in the pews.

With self-examination, encouraged and given precision by the iron-sharpening of our team members, we are able to battle individualism and hang together in community. In turn, our communities are able to more powerfully confront distorted hyper-communities like gangs. A marginalized population without resources, hope, pastors or Christ-centered leaders is a survival community. Each person is struggling to go forward in the individualism bequeathed from the dominant culture. Our communities, when they are healthy, live as a prophetic challenge to gangs, exhibiting the beauty of familial connectedness without the kind of allegiance that promotes rivalry and violence.

Joining InnerCHANGE, Servants or another fellowship of workers among the poor does not automatically mean we have subdued the demon of individualism. Often we simply channel the pride and self-reliance of individualism into communities and express it corporately as elitism. Historically, high-commitment communities have often been prone to attitudes of superior spirituality. We see it in Jesus' disciples. We have seen it in ourselves. In InnerCHANGE, we have organized as an order not because we are exceptional and desire to be elite, but because we are ordinary and desire to be effective.

At the other end of the spectrum from elitism is another pathology to which communities are vulnerable; we have christened it the *Nazareth Syndrome*. When Philip tells Nathanael about Jesus, Nathanael quips, "Can anything good come out of Nazareth?" (Jn 1:46 ESV). The Latin American proverb "There is no worse wedge than one taken from the same wood" reminds us that community members can reserve some of their worst opprobrium for one another, often expressing it in annihilating comments or critiques cloaked in "speaking the truth in love."[5] Again, the disciples are instructive for us. On Jesus' last evening with them before the cross, the disciples dissolve painfully into competitive bickering and backbiting—even after their feet have been washed.

We've seen in InnerCHANGE that the apparent opposites—elitism and internal diminishment—can, ironically, be expressed in community simultaneously. Perhaps that is because both spring out of insecurity. Humility is a remedy for these diseases, along with constant prayerful vigilance. We've found no reliable "hair shirt" to induce humility that fits all teams. C. S. Lewis, however, offers one way in a quotation attributed to him: "Humility isn't thinking less of yourself, it's thinking about yourself less." Communities often seek to create cohesion in sophisticated processes or rules, when the most efficient remedies for elitism or destructive criticism are often simply over-the-counter variations on the golden rule. Thankfully the wider community, composed of our neighbors, often gently schools us in humility. They help relieve us of the weighty burden of being the "perfect" community ministering to the "broken" ones.

THE CROWDS

In their missional journey to Nain, Jesus and his disciples are accompanied by a crowd. There they encounter a widow likewise accompanied by a crowd. In Luke's account, the disciples do not insist on a priority based on special calling or unique role; they do not elbow either crowd away.

If our apostolic communities grow impatient or discomfited

with the "crowd," we're operating with too narrow a definition of community and too limited a vision for the impact of the crowd. Luke 7:17 specifically tells us that the events at Nain were reported "through the whole of Judea and all the surrounding country." It is the crowd members who spread the news of the miracle at Nain. It is the crowd that extends the impact of the ministry. We must have eyes to see the value of the crowd. Much damage has been done when missionaries adopt the attitude that they are full-timers, professionally trained clergy, and that church members or bivocational local leaders are simply volunteers who minister for a season on their terms and go home.

The term *friar* conjures images of single, male clergy, deeply committed to community with one another. New friars are working to reimagine this wineskin in a way that retains the intensity of commitment to community characteristic of the historical friars, but broadens the expression to embrace multiple communities in a way that facilitates transformation in a neighborhood. Specifically, this means we commit to communities of team members, neighbors, Christian leaders and others whom God is drawing together to renew a community gripped with poverty. In its depiction of three interlocking communities gathered together around Christ—the disciples, the crowd with Jesus and the crowd with the widow—the story of Nain is particularly instructive, because it both resembles complex dynamics in our contexts and represents a helpful model of mutual appreciation.

It is fashionable to be discontented with the modern church, especially in its megachurch forms. Much of the critique is careful and helpful, but often it leads to an individualistic separation into communities that eschew old ones. And many of these new communities are discovering that it is not easy to survive on anti-message and designer disgruntlement. Churches all over the world, no matter how dowdy they can sometimes be, are still the bride of Christ. As high-commitment communities, we are called to collaborate with churches as well as with the broader Christian community. Collaboration can be tedious, but as Winston Churchill quipped, "There is only one thing worse than fighting with allies, and that is fighting without them."[6]

In this story, the communities gather as allies. They tailor themselves to the situation presented here: all face Christ as he experiences a moment of intimacy with a grieving mother, and around that centrality, all find an appropriate posture. In the presence of Christ, there is no better or worse posture. There is only facing or not facing him.

SUFFERING AND THE WITNESS OF "WITH-NESS"

"Not working on, or for, but with": this is how a Glasgow church planter and teacher, Wes White, recently unpacked the powerful phrase "witness of with-ness."[7] We find that many enter mission with a subconscious sense of going with the answers. Similarly, many are willing to *stand up* for people in poverty. But there are few who will *stand with* them. These emerging fellowships among the poor are those who are called to stand with. This powerful quotation grew out of Aboriginal activist work in Queensland in the 1970s: "If you have come to help me, you are wasting your time. But if you have come because your liberation is bound up with mine, then let us work together."[8] Community is such an important issue for us in InnerCHANGE that we have articulated it as both a value we hold dear and as a commitment we make to one another and our neighbors. It is both medium and message, a witness in and of itself. In his Gospel, John tells us that the world will know us by our love—something we dismiss too easily as a cliché.

TO STAND WITH THE WIDOW

Jesus and his disciples step into and not around the wailing mourners. And Jesus' choice to join the funeral procession brings about life. There are times we will not see new life when we join with the bereaved, but we can grieve with or on behalf of people in poverty who are experiencing great loss. One summer, on the Santa Ana street that was the birthplace of InnerCHANGE, our neighborhood lost three young men to gang violence in the space of six weeks. All three had hovered just outside our ministry orbit, and yet they were neighborhood "sons" with whom we shared a sense of belonging, woven into our lives as community. Instinctively we found ourselves grieving deeply, personally, alongside our neighbors. That summer we found that there were no words adequate for so terrible a loss, just a posture—the posture of being with the widow.

TO BE THE WIDOW

Then there are the sons who die that no one claims, and our new friar communities suffer alone. The InnerCHANGE team in Caracas is located in a *barrio* precariously perched on a hillside high above the city. This community, named Pedro Camejo, has been terrorized routinely by a number of very violent young men called *malandros*. Members of InnerCHANGE gradually grew in relationship with one of the most notorious *malandros* and shared the love of Christ with him. Eventually, in a spasm of vigilante justice, a group from the community tracked down this young man and killed him. Sadly, the day before, Ryan Mathis and a friend prayed for this young man and sensed they were anointing him with a special word from the Lord. Even though we endure the terror of gang violence along with our neighbors, we also suffer the grief of losing gang members we have come to know and love in the power of Christ. This grief is an emotion not usually shared by our neighbors. After the *malandro* friend was killed, the Caracas team found themselves radically out of step with a community that was, instead, relieved by his death.

TO BE THE SON

Then there is the son. He is also part of the community, and as ministers of good news, we may be bewildered to find ourselves in that role. No matter how compelling our vision, no matter how exciting our incarnational posture, no matter how life-giving our formation, sometimes we may find ourselves to be the son in the coffin. We may, at times, be flat-lined by burnout, disappointment or despair. Sometimes those seasons stretch on and on until we feel trapped by such hopelessness and helplessness that we find ourselves in a crawl space. We find ourselves to be the son, entombed.

What does it mean to be the son, present in community only in the gift of weakness? Los Angeles InnerCHANGE team member Catherine Rundle, who has journeyed with her husband through two battles with virulent lymphoma, writes:

> It has meant receiving help. It has meant turning to our neighbors for intercession. It has meant a deep awareness of how much kindness matters, especially kindness from

strangers. It has meant waiting. It has meant allowing people to form their first impression of us not from what we could do, but from who we are on our worst days. It has meant beginning our lives in the same way many of our neighbors began theirs, disoriented and overwhelmed. It has meant preaching the gospel without words.[9]

Some of us will wait and wait for breakthroughs in the desolation. We often suffer privately—remaining in community but with pain driving us inward to stare at the retinal wall of our interior lives. But we must struggle to remain in community, in plain sight. In the journey to Nain, the son is surrounded by those who love him. He is carried by community members intent on his welfare. And inside the coffin, however confining, he retains the dignity of being a son. And Jesus' love is always just a hand's breadth away.

Whatever posture we are privileged to assume in this story, whatever role in community we play, Jesus' love is real, and we are all absolutely dependent on it.

TOUCHING THE BIER

At one moment in this story from Luke, everything hangs in the balance. Jesus reaches out and touches the bier. Everything stops.

In a world with more than three billion people living on less than two dollars a day, experiencing a gripping poverty that buries widows' sons before their time, we are called as workers among the poor to stand with Christ and declare that this is not the world we want to live in. We are called to admit that those of us who are not poor are generally blind to those who are, because the seeing-eye dog of our dominant culture of self-ism and consumerism too easily leads us about. We are called to declare with kingdom confidence that the existence of poverty is not *just*, even when the world laments cynically that it is *just* reality.

All over the world there are funeral processions taking place like this one in Nain. As new friars, we are called to say that they are not all inevitable. Many, in fact, are interruptible as we journey communally under the leadership and power of Christ— if we will simply reach out and touch the bier.

Dave Everitt, member of InnerCHANGE Cambodia since 1994, tells a story of praying for a baby who had died in remote Mondulkiri Province. Dave is a natural evangelist, but the same impulse that took him into the most outlying and impoverished regions of the country also brought him into constant collision with the desperate medical needs of villagers. These men and women and their families simply could not afford to travel to one of the few government clinics in a substantial town. A trip could cost two weeks' income, and a clinic's fee could cost all their livestock.

In response, Dave apprenticed under several missionary physicians in Phnom Penh and eventually was commissioned as an evangelist, church planter and field medic. In a tiny hamlet called DuDou, while Dave and a church elder, Koy, were examining, treating and praying for a number of sick villagers, a frantic woman ran up to them. She was carrying a motionless baby girl in her arms. Dave writes:

> It was evening. The baby had been sick for several days with diarrhea, vomiting, and complete dehydration. When I examined her I could find no heartbeat, no respiration. Completely fixed pupils. She was dead. Koy and I prayed

and pleaded for God to restore the baby to her parents. The mom and dad took the baby away that night and we were all heartbroken.

Early the next morning, they brought the baby back to us. She was a completely different child. Fully plumped out, no sign of weakness or dehydration. She had returned to being a normal tickly and giggly infant. The mom said that during the night they had placed her dead body in a hammock, waiting to decide how to do her funeral the next morning after consulting with the elders. They woke to the sound of their daughter cooing and rustling in the hammock, fully alive, fully restored. We knew she had been dead the night before, no doubt. Then she was alive, no doubt, either.

Whose prayer did Jesus answer? One of us, or all of us—I don't know. It was my hands that were laid on her. It was her mom's tears that soaked her. Koy and the head elder prayed the loudest. Unity in the Body is the fragrance of grace.

As new friars we have the privilege of journeying with Jesus in places at the world's margins, like Nain. Along the way we will encounter and experience the deep well of emotion of the widow, the cleansing grief of the mourners, the solidarity of the bearers, the hopeful expectation of the crowd, the camaraderie of the disciples and perhaps, even, the desolation and consolation of the son. And if we have clear eyes to take in the full measure of community, we will discover that the journey is truly more "we" than "me." And that will be transforming.

Epilogue

CHALLENGES AND POSSIBILITIES FOR A NEW GENERATION OF MISSION WORKERS

Ash Barker

Behold, I am making all things new.

REVELATION 21:5

Though we may draw inspiration from the first Christians and the likes of St. Francis and others who sought to be both relevant to their changing worlds and faithful to Jesus, this generation of mission workers must find our own, new voice. "Behold, I am making all things new" can be a kind of promise from God for this generation, because our unique context requires new things of us. While we share much in common with the struggles every generation has faced, the thing which has struck me about the remarkable insights from this book are two common themes that this generation of workers is grappling with, issues which are quite distinct from previous generations: incarnation and urbanization.

A NEW UNDERSTANDING OF THE INCARNATIONAL APPROACH

Some people think that because my wife, Anji, and I moved our family into Klong Toey slum in Bangkok, Thailand, we are therefore "incarnational"—we have somehow become the "same as" our poor neighbors. However, just look into the wide eyes of little Lek and you will see this is not possible.[1]

Lek is a four-year-old girl, smiling a toothless grin through the dirt on her face and matted hair, her tiny hand wrapped around our son Aiden's plastic action figure on our floor. Surely the blood-stained spots on her ripped dress and dark purple bruises on her arms and back tell me I cannot even imagine identifying with her. With her formative stages of life so dislocated, Lek's foundations have already been undermined before they've really begun. I mean, even Jesus couldn't be the "same as" little Lek—and he *was* the incarnation!

Anji takes up this struggle with all its complexities in her reflection on Lek.

> The day before Christmas, our daughter Amy and I cried out to God as we heard and saw through the slat windows our neighbor beating his little girl over and over with a stick. The assault went on for 25 minutes and we struggled with wanting to intervene to make it stop, knowing that getting involved would make the assault worse as the father would then lose face. There were other neighbors around who also looked shocked and struggled to know how to make it stop. It was wrong that we did not inter-

vene, it is wrong that the culture values saving face over the safety of little children, and it was wrong that as a Christian I failed to act regardless of the consequences.

Talking with senior Thais later, they explained that only someone older than the father could intervene and that if a westerner got involved this would bring great shame resulting in a worse beating when we were not there. I am not sure how we should have intervened, but I am faced with the uncomfortable fact that I let a small child be abused and should have acted. Everything is connected and, yes, my actions would have impacted the neighborhood. The catalyst for the beating was that the dad had been yelled at for owing money to another neighbor. He lost face and took his shame out on his little girl. Lek's Mum sat by washing the dishes and Amy and I sat by crying out to God to make it stop. Maybe God was waiting for me to stop it?

We are trying to bring the hope of Christ into the chaos that is our neighborhood. This has got to be word, deed and sign. One of the up sides of being packed in together is the amazing opportunity to do life with lots of people. This is not always difficult, and is often joyous and hopeful. At times it is even miraculous when God allows us to be part of His work in our neighbor's lives. The fact remains that those joyous times cannot be accessed without also being part of the horrible times. So in that I seek comfort, the hopelessness is never a long lasting feeling but a very necessary one as I try to live consistently as a servant of God—something I don't always succeed at but hope to keep improving upon. The promise of Christ for us all is that His Kingdom WILL come on earth and I strive forward towards that end, seeing little glimpses of it here each day.[2]

If we can't really be the "same as" Lek (and of course neither Lek nor I can be the "same as" Jesus in so many ways), it could then be easily assumed that an attempt at incarnational mission is simply costly and misguided. Jesus was the *incartio* ("made flesh"), as in "The Word became flesh and blood and moved into the neighborhood" (Jn 1:14 *The Message*). When applied to us in the way it was used to describe God become human, the metaphor of enfleshment has real limits.

I prefer the term *relocation* to *incarnation* as one of the marks of new friars. None of the new friars who move from Western suburbs into slums would want to identify the suburbs as heaven or themselves as messiahs, and they would admit their inability to become like the poor in the ways God became like us in Christ. Incarnation is not something we do, as if rich persons could incarnate into poor persons. Rather, we are inspired and informed by the incarnation of God in Christ and apply this act of God to inform and inspire our five marks: incarnational relocation, incarnational devotion, incarnational community living, incarnational mission and incarnational solidarity on the margins. Few Christians would consider devotion, community, mission, relocation and solidarity in and of themselves distinct from other generations of mission workers. It is *incarnation* that makes these marks new in our movement. And it is *hope* that becomes enfleshed in these marks.

It is worth noting that incarnational relocation also describes those who return to slums after leaving them for a time. Due to

the inspiration of Christ's incarnation, the place of such returners in the community has changed. They are located anew as
incarnations of hope.[3]

The risen Christ invites us to follow, join and participate with
him in enfleshing his kingdom on earth as in heaven. As we
take up this invitation we don't become mini-gods, special people or the same as those suffering. But we do begin to uncover
the presence of Christ in our neighborhoods, and we enflesh—
or make real—the promises of God. Such enfleshed hope can
change the trajectory of people's lives and advance the whole of
creation's redemptive destiny. This is the good news we have to
offer the Leks of the world: a new kingdom can come alive and
be seen now "in the flesh" through us, even as we wait for the
complete fulfillment of all God's promises.

This not an easy approach to take. As Urban Neighbours of
Hope workers we covenant together to "share our lives and resources in solidarity with those living in urban poverty." Urban
poverty is far more painful and awkward for little Lek than I
could ever experience. In the parable of the sheep and the goats
("As you do it to the least of these, you do it to me," Mt 25:31-
46) we are promised that we can meet Jesus in poverty and human suffering, and find dynamism for transformation and hope.
Any of the hard and awkward experiences of living up close and
personal with those in need is nothing compared to the sense of
purpose and meaning infused in us as we watch hope rise in
lives of the little Leks of our neighborhoods. Martin Luther
King Jr. said in his 1963 speech from the Lincoln Memorial in
Washington, D.C., that "unearned suffering is redemptive." Relocating to a slum home is a small price to pay for the privilege
of enfleshing hope.

Incarnation-inspired relocation is very different from the colonization, empire building and institution-centered missions of past eras. We have seen the failures of these and are determined to find more Christ-centered ways forward. We simply don't want to dominate the world. Our groups are not the incarnate Lord. Only Jesus is Lord. We recognize that organizational and community disciplines are crucially important for sustainability, but even this cannot be the main focus. We instead give our best personal and organizational attention to participating with Christ in the slums, since he has already "moved into the neighborhood."

An incarnational approach, then, is not one special method or model. Rather it's about living in ways that detect and enflesh the special presence of the risen Jesus. No matter where we're called to live, I pray we can all find ways to join and make real the hope only found in the incarnation—the crucified and living Lord Jesus Christ, who invites us all to "come, follow me." To follow, join and participate with this Christ is to find our true lives.

RELOCATING IN A NEW URBANIZED CENTURY

Since Scott Bessenecker's book *The New Friars: The Emerging Movement Among the World's Poor* was published, two anonymous people quietly tipped the balance of human history. The first person was either born or moved into an urban area sometime in late 2007, and for the first time in human history, more people were living in urban than rural areas.[4] The world is urbanizing at a pace the planet has never seen before.

In 1800, only 3 percent of humans lived in urban areas. That number had increased to 14 percent by 1900 and 30 by 1950.[5]

Now it is projected that urban dwellers will reach 5 billion, or 61 percent of the population, by 2030.[6] One UN report says:

> Virtually all the population increase expected during 2000-2030 world level concentrates in urban areas. Ninety-five per cent of the population increase expected during 2000-2030 will be absorbed by the urban areas of the less developed regions whose populations will likely rise from approximately 2 billion in 2000 to just under 3.5 billion in 2030.[7]

It is no exaggeration therefore to describe the twenty-first century, as authors Jo Beall and Sean Fox do, as our planet's "first urban century."[8]

The world has changed irreversibly, not just because the majority of new population growth will now happen in these urban areas generally, but because this growth will occur in urban slum and squatter neighborhoods of low-income countries more specifically. And this was exactly what our second anonymous person did to tip the scales of human history. Sometime in 2005 the one-billionth person was born or moved into an urban slum and squatter neighborhood.[9]

To put this into context, consider that when Christ commanded the first disciples to "go into all the world," the planet only had about 200 million people. It took humanity until 1804 to reach one billion in global population.[10] And with the population now roughly 6 billion, that one-billionth slum dweller means that as of 2005 one in every six humans is living in a slum.[11] The number of slum dwellers could double within twenty years, meaning that by 2030 one in four people—the entire world population as recently as 1930[12]—might be living in urban slums.[13] Though with so many variables, not least of which include diseases and technologies yet unknown, long-term population growth is notoriously difficult to predict. The fact that some UN estimates have over half the world living in urban slums by 2050[14] should get the world's best attention—not least the best attention from this generation of Jesus-followers.

It is right in the middle of these morphing and moving settings that most of the insights in this book are written. That includes me, who for the last eight years has lived with my family in the largest urban slum and squatter neighborhood in Bangkok, and before that in one of Melbourne's poorest urban neighborhoods for over ten years. These are the local arenas that will shape the world as we go forward. This is radically different from the predominately rural world of our forebears. New technologies are changing the face of agricultural labor, forcing people to emigrate from anywhere in order to go anywhere to find work. Advances in health care have enabled more people to live longer. Add to this the flattening of the world with globalization fueled by access to cheap travel and instant connectedness, and we have a world that is changing faster and becoming more vulnerable than ever before. This world is one requiring new wineskins.

Like most around the world, our slum has no protection from the law and could therefore be bulldozed at any moment. Other similar nearby neighborhoods have been demolished, legally. Though our slum has over eighty thousand residents in two square kilometers and has survived since the 1930s, it might continue on or it might not. Traditional and conventional mission, church growth and development theories tested and perfected in stable, rural settings, with a focus on sustainability and institu-

tion capacity building, suddenly become irrelevant in such a setting. A new generation of Jesus-followers needs to adapt, build
trust and use multiple strategies at speeds and in ways that could
not have been envisioned even a decade ago. The new friars, from
their homes living on the front line of urban poverty, are in the
best place to accomplish this new work in Jesus' name.

FROM GOOD INTENTIONS TO MOVEMENTS

My final reflections here are inherent challenges we face as
those growing up in globalization. We become used to the instant, individualized choices and the dramatic and ecstatic experiences that we can easily access. The problem is that what is
required from us at this time is radically different from what
we've accustomed ourselves to. The virtues and habits required,
like patience, humility, love, faith, hope, community building
and Christ-centeredness (as opposed to self-centeredness) do
not come naturally to those of us who've grown up in this world
of instant gratification. They are not easily or quickly developed either.

We have to be honest and say that while we long for a movement like the one St. Francis saw, with hundreds of thousands
personally involved (it would be millions with today's demographic equivalent), we are not there yet. Not even close, actually. There are less than a few hundred of us new friars currently
living in poor, urban, developing world neighborhoods and
committing more than a year or two of our lives to this vocation—far short of what is required in the slums and urban-poor
neighborhoods of this world today, never mind in the coming
years. The new seeds of revolution may well be planted, but they
have barely sprouted.

Can I share my biggest fear in contributing to a book like this? It's not that people won't like the book, or won't care about this work, or won't have good intentions. I see enough goodwill everywhere I go to appreciate the sympathetic response. What I fear most is that people will read this book and live vicariously through the few of us who are already out there and overwhelmed by what is in front of us. Reading is not the same as living your faith, and we inoculate you to your call if this happens. It reminds me of Elias Chacour, a Palestinian priest who got a scholarship to leave occupied Palestine and go to France for seminary and university education. He would have many choices about where to invest his life afterward. A professor gave Elias and his class this advice:

> "If there is a problem somewhere" he said with his dry chuckle, "this is what happens. Three people will try to do something concrete to settle the issue. Ten people will give a lecture analyzing what the three are doing. One hundred people will commend or condemn the ten for their lecture. One thousand people will argue about the problem. And one person—only one—will involve themselves so deeply in the true solution that they are too busy to listen to any of it." Now asking gently, his penetrating eyes meeting each of ours in turn, "which person are you?"

Elias would go back to his homeland in occupied Palestine to serve his people by building schools, hospitals and churches for over fifty years. He would become the archbishop of Galilee and an ambassador for nonviolence in the way of Jesus.

Which person will you be? Will you step out as new friars or just stand on the sidelines formulating opinions? Please step out and act before the new seeds that have been planted are choked to death by the cares of the world and the deceitfulness of wealth.

We know we can do this new work through Christ because it has been done via other means by previous generations. It's our turn now to see all things made new. Can there be a better way to spend our lives than focusing our best imagination, resources and time on this living mission?

Notes

Foreword

[1]Population estimates for slum communities are difficult to render given the informal nature of the housing and the rapidity with which they are growing. Estimates for slum dwellers in the first several years of the twenty-first century range roughly from one to two billion individuals.

[2]Mike Davis, *Planet of Slums* (London: Verso, 2006), p. 22.

Chapter 1: A New Wineskin

[1]*Majority world* refers to the portions of our planet, previously known as the *third world* and sometimes called the *developing world* or *global south*, which make up the majority of human population.

[2]John T. McNeill, *The Celtic Churches: A History*, A.D. 200 to 1200 (Chicago: University of Chicago Press, 1974), p. 225

[3]"Religion: A Challenge from Evangelicals," *Time*, August 5, 1974 <www .time.com/time/magazine/article/0,9171,879423-1,00.html>.

[4]Philip Jenkins, *The Next Christendom: The Coming of Global Christianity* (Oxford: Oxford University Press, 2002).

[5]Chris Heuertz, "Subverting Evangelicalism," *The Other Journal* 8, no. 17 (2006) <www.theotherjournal.com/article.php?id=209>.

[6]Kenneth Scott Latourette, *A History of Christianity* (New York: HarperCollins, 1975), p. 375.

[7]Ibid., p. 377.

[8]Ibid., p. 405.

[9]Ibid., p. 406.

[10]See the reflections from Howard Brandt on the Oscar Muriu lectures at "News from SIM East and Southern Africa" <http://simesafrica.blogspot .com/2008/09/oscar-muriu-lectures.html>.

[11]There are four major Catholic orders that use the designation *friar*: Dominican, Franciscan, Carmelite and Augustinian.

Chapter 2: Hovering Spirit, Creative Voice, Empowered Transformation

[1]"The Lifestyle and Values of Servants" was drafted in 1981 with significant influence from the Rule of Taizé and the Anglican Franciscan rule. It is included in Viv Grigg, *Cry of the Urban Poor* (Milton Keynes, U.K.: Authentic, 2004), chap. 7.

[2]Viv Grigg, *Servants Movements: Protestant Missionary Orders with Vows of Non-Destitute Poverty* (Auckland, N.Z.: Urban Leadership Foundation, 1985); and a brief paper that is now the basis of a chapter in Viv Grigg, *The Spirit of Christ and the Postmodern City* (Lexington, Ky.: Emeth Press, 2009). I did not publish these widely as I had an intuitive feeling that misunderstandings about orders may cause workers to return to an ancient Catholicism or monasticism, which had the potential of destroying the very apostolic liberty that the pentecostal St. Francis had sought to foster.

[3]Roy is a pseudonym.

[4]This would presumably include roughly five thousand from each continent, including North America.

Chapter 3: Incarnational

[1]According to UNICEF, one billion people worldwide lack access to clean drinking water (www.nesc.wvu.edu/ndwc/articles/OT/FA06/OT_Fl_06_NNweb.pdf).

[2]Diarrhea and the resulting dehydration are responsible for about two million child deaths every year across the world <www.vancouversun.com/health/Salt+sugar+water+avert+diarrhea+deaths/1374179/story.html>.

[3]At the same time, one of the members of our team, physician Susan Jack, was working with NGOs to advocate a law that would ban milk powder companies from advertising. This law was passed in 2006. This is a good example of the partnership between grassroots, microlevel mission and a more policy-oriented, macrolevel approach.

[4]"Vancouver a Scarred Paradise, UN Says," *Vancouver Sun,* June 28, 2007 <www.canada.com/vancouversun/story.html?id=2acd99cd-3017-47ce-8e49-437d83bd7411&k=61909>.

[5]We tend to castigate the poor who are closest to us as a way of avoiding engagement with them. In the "centers," we have the luxury of demonizing and dispensing with the poor; but by living and engaging on the margins, the poor become our community, and so their struggles are part of our burden.

[6]Kofi Annan, foreword to United Nations Settlement Programme, *The Challenge of Slums: Global Report on Urban Settlements 2003* (London: Earth-

scan, 2003), p. v <www.unhabitat.org/downloads/docsGRHS.2003.0.pdf>.

[7]Nate Buchanan, "Changing the Story of Change," *Geez Magazine* 15, fall 2009 <www.geezmagazine.org/issue15/changing-the-story-of-change>.

[8]Buchanan continues with his critique of new monasticism explaining, "The second mark [of new monasticism] is sharing economic resources with fellow community members and the needy among us." The needy aren't us, he points out: "The community isn't made up of the needy but rather the people who organize themselves to serve the needy." His point is that our missiology is rarely from the perspective of the poor. Even the third mark, "hospitality to the stranger," assumes that the stranger, the one in need of hospitality, is not the protagonist in the story.

[9]This is evidenced by the fact that most of us new friar types reject the label "missionary."

[10]The roots of this insecurity are complex. Partly it is a natural reaction against wrong emphases in the past. Yet somehow we must avoid the theological equivalent of throwing the baby out with the bathwater. For more on this, see Craig Greenfield, "Desperately Needed: More Outsiders—A Biblical Mandate for Cross-Cultural Missions," June 19, 2009 <www.servants asia.org/index.php?option=com_content&view=article&id=402%3Adesp erately-needed-more-outsiders-a-biblical-mandate-for-cross-cultural-missi ons&catid=8%3Ageneral&Itemid=16&lang=en>.

[11]We find this ironic, since many of these technical advisors are paid disproportionately high salaries and live in expensive houses paid for by the NGOs and governments that subscribe to this approach.

[12]Our attitude should be the same as that of Jesus Christ, who didn't grasp after his rightful place in heaven but instead humbled himself and took on the very nature of a servant (paraphrased from Phil 2:5-7).

[13]The ministry is called Kinbrace Community, and it comes under the umbrella of Salsbury Community Society.

[14]In some ways the biblical role of the prophet is always to be an "outsider" rejected by the community (Lk 4:24). These two roles are intricately bound up together.

[15]For example, in our Western cultures the church has almost universally sold out to the dominant cultural values of getting ahead, accumulating wealth and pursuing comfort. Developed countries need these prophetic strangers as much as any other country.

[16]For example, Servants workers commit to refrain from starting any new ministry initiatives in their first twelve months, which are dedicated to language and cultural learning.

[17]"Moses" comes from the Egyptian word *mos*, which means child.

[18]Other returners in the Bible include Nehemiah, the high-powered, government-sanctioned returner; Naomi, the low-powered refugee returner; and Ezra, the theologian returner.

[19]Likewise in John 1:11: "He came to that which was his own, but his own did not receive him."

[20]Craig Greenfield, "Report from Tsunami Ground Zero," January 9, 2005 <www.servantsasia.org/index.php?option=com_content&view=article&id=154%3Aalias-of-news-with-id154&catid=8%3Ageneral&Itemid=16&lang=en>.

[21]This can be either positive or negative: positive, when the emotions motivate toward thoughtful action, and negative, when emotions take priority over reason and you lose your sense of perspective.

[22]John B. Hayes, in personal correspondence via e-mail, July 15, 2009.

[23]Viv Grigg, Companion to the Poor: Christ in the Urban Slums (Kansas City: MARC Publications, 1990), p. 204.

Chapter 4: Missional

[1]World Bank, 1990 report on urban policy and economic development, quoted in José Luis Corragio, "Human Capital: The World Bank's Approach to Education in Latin America," accessed May 4, 2010, at <www.coraggioeconomia.org/jlc/archivos%20para%20descargar/Human_Capital.doc>.

[2]According to Philip Jenkins in his landmark piece The Next Christendom (New York: Oxford University Press, 2002), in about forty years 80 percent of the world's Christians will be non-Western and non-white. God's kingdom is rapidly expanding throughout the majority world!

[3]Darrow Miller and Bob Moffitt, On Earth As It Is in Heaven (Tioga, N.D.: Harvest Publishing, 2005), p. vi.

[4]Melba Padilla Maggay, Transforming Society (London: SPCK, 1994), pp. 20, 68, 141.

[5]Bob Moffitt, If Jesus Were Mayor (Apex, N.C.: Monarch Books, 2007), p. 28.

[6]Quoted by Tim Costello, in Neil Cole, Organic Church (San Francisco: Jossey-Bass, 2005), p. 123.

[7]Mohandas Gandhi, quoted on Otium Sanctum <http://otiumsanctum.com/2009/03/09/ghandi-on-the-bible/>.

[8]By framing narrative we mean the way we see the world, the way we see ourselves, the way we think and feel about our surroundings; the hopes we have, the longings we have. Who we are, where we are, what we are, what will give us meaning and purpose, what we should live for: all these are

questions answered by our framing narratives or underlying storylines.

[9]See Miller and Moffitt, *On Earth As It Is in Heaven.*

[10]See, for example, Perry B. Yoder, *Shalom: The Bible's Word of Salvation, Justice, and Peace* (Newton, Kans.: Faith and Life Press, 1987), p. 9. See also Arthur F. Glasser, *Announcing the Kingdom* (Grand Rapids: Baker Academic, 2003), p. 130; Bryant Myers, *Walking with the Poor* (Maryknoll, N.Y.: Orbis, 1999); and Robert Linthicum, *City of God, City of Satan* (Grand Rapids: Zondervan, 1991).

[11]The judgment we see falling on them is more passive than active. It is God no longer intervening, no longer protecting, but instead withdrawing and letting the consequences of their action fall on their own heads. See, for example, Ezekiel 22:31.

[12]N.T. Wright, *Simply Christian: Why Christianity Makes Sense* (New York: HarperSanFrancisco, 2006), pp. 217, 219.

[13]John Eldredge, *Epic: The Story God Is Telling* (Nashville: Thomas Nelson, 2007), pp. 87, 93, 98.

[14]Darrell Johnson, *Discipleship on the Edge* (Vancouver, B.C.: Regent College Publishing, 2004), p. 362.

[15]Martin Luther King Jr., *Strength to Love* (Philadelphia: Fortress, 1981), p. 18.

[16]Martin Luther King Jr., "Letter from a Birmingham Jail" <www.africa.u penn.edu/Articles_Gen/Letter_Birmingham.html>.

[17]Martin Luther, quoted by Rafael Seligmann in "An Apple Tree Against Sadness: What Is the Root of German Melancholy? A Study of Souls," in *The Atlantic Times,* March 2006 <www.atlantic-times.com/archive_detail .php?recordID=459>.

Chapter 5: Marginal

[1]For example, God identifies with those who are poor (Prov 14:31; 17:5; 19:17; Is 3:14-15); God establishes reciprocal relationships for those available to the needs of friends who are poor (Deut 15:4; Ps 41:1; Prov 21:13; 22:9); God validates the authenticity of our Christian virtue in relationship with poor people (Prov 19:17; 21:13, 22.9, 28:5; 29:7; Is 28:17; 58:6-11; Jer 22:16; Jas 2:5; 1 Jn 3:16-18); God uses the poor as a standard for judgment (Mt 25:36-39).

[2]Referring to poor people as "the poor" overidentifies them with their poverty. In an effort to use language more creatively and redemptively (and because we are usually speaking and writing about people we know rather than abstractions), we refuse to label people as "the poor" and instead refer to "our friends who are poor."

[3]For an explication on these categories of poverty, see Chris Heuertz, "What

Do We Mean by Poverty?" *The Cry* 8, no. 3 (2002), pp. 4-7 <www.word madeflesh.org/files/2009/04/fall2002.pdf>.

[4]John D. Zizioulas, *Being as Communion* (Yonkers, N.Y.: St. Vladimir's Seminary Press, 1997), p. 18.

[5]Jean Vanier, *From Brokenness to Community* (Mahwah, N.J.: Paulist Press, 1992), p. 20.

[6]The term "multitudes" found in the Gospels, especially Mark, refers to the *ochlos*, which denotes sinners, the excluded, the impoverished and the disinherited. This is the preferred audience of the message of the kingdom. Jesus calls the people to the way of the cross (Mk 8:34), teaches them (Mk 7:14), has compassion for them (Mk 6:34), heals them (Mk 1:34) and identifies with them (Mk 3:34). The *ochlos* are the primary addressees of Jesus' gospel, and the kingdom is revealed among them.

[7]Jürgen Moltmann, *The Church in the Power of the Spirit* (Minneapolis: Fortress, 1993), p. 127.

[8]A version of the following story also appeared on the Lausanne blog; see Noah Tullay, "God's Reign: An Invitation to Partnership," November 6, 2009 <www.lausanne.org/lausanne-blog/gods-reign-an-invitation-to-partnership.html>.

[9]Philip Jenkins, *The Next Christendom: The Coming of Global Christianity* (Oxford: Oxford University Press, 2002), p. 2.

[10]Walter Brueggemann, *The Threat of Life* (Minneapolis: Fortress, 1996), p. 45.

[11]Miroslav Volf, "Soft Difference: Theological Reflections on the Relation Between Church and Culture in 1 Peter," *Ex Auditu* 10 (1994): 15-17 <www.yale.edu/faith/resources/x_volf_difference.html>.

[12]Danielle R. Speakman, "Identity and Its Contribution to Resilience in Peruvian Street Youth" (dissertation, Fuller Theological Seminary, 2005).

Chapter 6: Devotional

[1]Thomas Keating, *The Human Condition: Contemplation and Transformation* (Mahwah, N.J.: Paulist Press, 1999), p. 41.

[2]Mother Teresa, *Total Surrender* (Ann Arbor, Mich.: Servant, 1985), p. 107.

[3]Henri Nouwen, *Beloved: Henri Nouwen in Conversation* (Grand Rapids: Eerdmans, 2007), p. 23.

[4]Thomas Keating, "Invitation to Love," in *Foundations for Centering Prayer and the Christian Contemplative Life* (New York: Continuum, 2002), chap. 1.

[5]Nouwen, *Beloved*, p. 23.

[6]Henri Nouwen, *Compassion: A Reflection on the Christian Life* (London: Darton, Longman & Todd, 2008), p. 112.

⁷*Lectio divina* is Latin for "sacred reading," though a more accurate definition might be "sacred listening." *Lectio divina* is a slow, contemplative praying of the Scriptures. Traditionally one progresses through the movements
of *lectio* (reading/listening), *meditatio* (meditation), *oratio* (prayer) and
ends with *contemplatio* (contemplation). These traditional Latin movements are also associated in this manner: *lectio* (acquaintanceship), *meditatio* (friendly companionship), *oratio* (friendship) and *contemplatio* (union).
For more information, see M. Basil Pennington, *Lectio Divina: Renewing
the Ancient Practice of Praying the Scriptures* (Chestnut Ridge, N.Y.: Crossroad, 1998).

Chapter 7: Communal
¹Richard Rohr, *Everything Belongs* (Chestnut Ridge, N.Y.: Crossroad, 1999),
p. 19.
²Sergio Torres and Virginia Febella, eds., *The Emergent Gospel: Theology
from the Developing World* (Maryknoll, N.Y.: Orbis, 1978), p. 7.
³Bobby Clinton, remark made in Transformational Leadership class at Fuller
Theological Seminary, June 1994.
⁴The same might be said of multigenerational teams and teams with diver-
sity in theology, gender, economic status, education, etc.
⁵Latin American proverb quoted in Justo Gonzalez, *Acts: The Gospel of the
Spirit* (Maryknoll, N.Y.: Orbis, 2001), p. 103.
⁶Quoted in William Manchester, *The Last Lion: Winston Spencer Churchill,
Alone* (Boston: Little, Brown, 1988), p. 632.
⁷Wes White, International Christian College in Glasgow, September 4,
2009. White told me (John) later that the phrase emerged in a brainstorm-
ing session with Brian McLaren in May 2008. (I should note here that I
have slightly changed the phrase to read "witness *of* with-ness.")
⁸Jone Johnson Lewis, Wisdom Quotes: Quotations to Inspire and Challenge
<www.wisdomquotes.com/cat_community.html>. This quote is often at-
tributed to Lila Watson, who in turn stated she was "not comfortable being
credited for something that had been born of a collective process." The quotation used here is one she accepts.
⁹Newsletter from Alastair and Catherine Rundle, April 2009.

Epilogue
¹"Lek" is a pseudonym.
²Anji Barker, "What Hope Do We Have to Offer?" in Ash and Anji Barker,
Finding Life: Reflections from a Bangkok Slum (Melbourne: UNOH, 2010),
p. 4.

[3]I am reluctant to include "remainers" here (see chapter three), although they can certainly incarnationally relocate themselves within their community. Too often outside organizations gobble up locals and graft them into their ranks, a modern act of colonialism.

[4]UN Habitat, *State of the World's Cities 2006/7* (London: Earthscan, 2006), pp. vii, x.

[5]Population Reference Bureau, "Human Population: Urbanization" <www.prb.org/Educators/TeachersGuides/HumanPopulation/Urbanization.aspx>.

[6]UN Habitat, *State of the World's Cities 2006/7*, p. vii.

[7]UN Habitat, *Slums of the World* (Nairobi: UN Habitat, 2003), p. 10.

[8]Jo Beall and Sean Fox, *Cities and Development* (New York: Routledge, 2009), Kindle loc. 421-48. See also UN Habitat, which describes the twenty-first century as "the urban century": Habitat Partner University Network (August 2009) <www.unhabitat.org/content.asp?typeid=19&catid=570&cid=6002>.

[9]UN Habitat, *State of the World's Cities 2006/7*, p. 19.

[10]Matt Rosenberg, "Current World Population: Current World Population and World Population Growth Since the Year One," accessed February 2, 2010, <http://geography.about.com/od/obtainpopulationdata/a/worldpopulation.htm>.

[11]UN Habitat, *The Challenge of Slums* (London: Earthscan, 2003), p. iv.

[12]Rosenberg, "Current World Population" <http://geography.about.com/od/obtainpopulationdata/a/worldpopulation.htm>.

[13]Ibid., p. xxiv.

[14]Alex Kirby, "Slum growth 'shames the world'" (October 2003) <http://news.bbc.co.uk/2/hi/science/nature/3161812.stm>.

About the Contributors

Ash Barker is international director of Urban Neighbors of Hope. He's written many books, including *Make Poverty Personal* and *Surrender All*.

Scott Bessenecker is associate director of missions for Inter-Varsity Christian Fellowship/USA. He is the author of *The New Friars* and *How to Inherit the Earth*.

David Chronic lives in Romania, where he serves as regional director of Word Made Flesh for Europe and Africa.

Derek Engdahl is general director and field director of Servant Partners (www.servantpartners.org). He lives in Pomona, California.

Craig and Nayhouy Greenfield together established Project Halo and Big Brothers and Sisters ministries in Phnom Penh, Cambodia. Craig is international coordinator of Servants to Asia's Urban Poor (www.servantsasia.org) and the author of *The Urban Halo*.

Viv Grigg coordinates the Encarnação Alliance of urban poor movement leaders. He is the author of many books, including *Companion to the Poor* and *Spirit of Christ and the Postmodern City.*

John B. Hayes is general director of InnerCHANGE (www .crmleaders.org/ministries/innerchange) and author of *Sub-Merge.*

Phileena and Christopher L. Heuertz are coexecutive directors of Word Made Flesh (www.wordmadeflesh.org). Phileena is the author of *Pilgrimage of a Soul;* Chris is author of *Simple Spirituality* and coauthor of *Friendship at the Margins.*

Jean-Luc Krieg is field director for Servant Partners in Mexico City (www.servantpartners.org) and executive director of Transformacion Urbana Internacional.

José Peñate-Aceves lives in San Francisco, where he serves as codirector of Communidad San Dimas for InnerCHANGE (www.crmleaders.org/ministries/innerchange).

Darren Prince is director of member formation for Inner-CHANGE. He lives in London.